Trash Your Debt

Trash Your Debt

✦

A Real-Life Story and How-To Guide
for Getting Out of Debt
and Becoming Financially Stable

Arnold D. Fredrick

iUniverse, Inc.
New York Lincoln Shanghai

Trash Your Debt
A Real-Life Story and How-To Guide for Getting Out of Debt and Becoming Financially Stable

iUniverse books may be ordered through booksellers or by contacting:

iUniverse
2021 Pine Lake Road, Suite 100
Lincoln, NE 68512
www.iuniverse.com
1-800-Authors (1-800-288-4677)

First Printing Edition
Images by Clipart.com, used with permission

ISBN: 0-595-33723-6

Printed in the United States of America

Contents

Author's Preface

I was just married, unemployed, and $34,000 in debt. My wife had a credit score of less than 300, many outstanding debts, and was also unemployed. After we had both become employed, our expenses still exceeded our monthly income. Six years have now passed. Both credit scores are now up. The $34,000 has long since been paid off. How is this possible, you ask? They must have had some special training or super education that allowed them to get a high-paying job. Actually, I have a high school diploma and have attended only four college classes. My first job after being married was as a youth director at a local church. My wife found a job as a customer-service rep for a local office-furniture store. She has a four-year degree from Purdue University in retail marketing.

The success I have achieved is from much study and applied common sense. That is how I know that you can also achieve what I have. It's called

Getting out of Debt!

Currently I am employed with a janitorial-supply company, and my wife is a customer-service rep for a worldwide company.

1

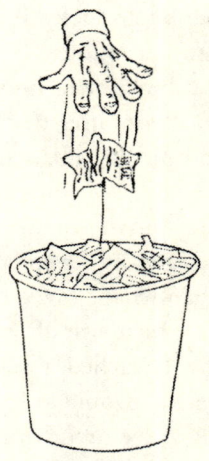

*Trash
Your
Debt
(Part 1)*

Chapter 1:
Trash Your Debt (Part 1)

There I was, just an average happy-go-lucky Joe living my life. Every dollar I made went right back out of my account. That is, *if* I even placed it in my account. The fact was, no matter how much money I made, I spent it all. Then one day I applied for a car loan. Soon after that new loan, numerous offers for credit cards followed. Of course I did the smart thing and said *yes* to all of them! Now don't get me wrong. I was not ever going to max them out. I just wanted options when it came to making purchases. So now every dollar I made went right back out, and I still owed money at the end of the year to my credit cards. It would seem that I spent more than what I made that year. So I figured, "I'll fix it the next year." Or should I say the next year after that?

Well, after a few years of this, I reached a huge decision in my life. So I did what any young and stupid person would do. I quit my job without having another job to go to. During my three-month time of looking for a job, I asked and married the longtime love of my life. This, unbeknownst to me, would be the greatest decision of my life. Of course the wedding ring, honeymoon, and all other living expenses were paid for by my many credit cards.

Now I must admit that, as of the date of my wedding, a company was in the midst of deciding whether to hire me. My wife had just quit her job in preparation for our move to the town of my new job. She also cleaned out her bank account that totaled $420, saying, "I trust you with all my money." When my new wife and I arrived back at her parents' house after the honeymoon, as my then current luck would have it, my new father-in-law had the pleasure of telling me that the company had called. They had decided not to hire me and was going to keep looking. I must admit that was a nice awkward moment for us.

So we moved into a room at my older brother's home. (The word small just does not do justice in describing our new home.) Two more months went by before a job found me. And so two more months of expenses just piled on top of my now well-used credit cards. The new job was a good job, but it required us to move. So, needless to say, even more expenses were paid by my now very well-used credit cards, some of which were maxed out.

We found an apartment we liked and somehow thought we could afford. I started my new job, and my wife started to look for a job. I am happy to report that she found one—just one month after we moved into our new apartment. So some (not all) living expenses went on the few cards that had available credit left. Now we were a two-income family, and we could start getting our finances in order. As I began to review and take count of where we were with our finances, this is what I found. I had one car loan with a balance of $11,000, many credit cards that totaled about $18,000, and a leftover hospital bill of $5,000. My wife had no outstanding debts, or so I thought until we looked at her credit report. There were many small outstanding bills that totaled about $600 and a credit score that was in the mid to high 200s. We only had one car for the two of us. Finally our new budget showed that after paying current bills and the minimum due on all credit cards there was about $25 per two weeks for food. Oh, but that was before I took out the money for our tithe. Now we were about, give or take, $100 in the hole every two weeks.

Many times along this journey of life I have looked back in stunned disbelief, asking if it was really that bad. How could we have ever gotten out of that hole alive? In this book I am going to tell you how we did it and, most importantly, how you can do it too. All my life growing up there were three goals or dreams that never left my thoughts. They were to be a youth minister, to play in a Christian rock band, and to be a millionaire. I still do not understand why these thoughts were so often in my head, but I knew I would accomplish these things someday. Needless to say, as a newlywed I was not thinking that whole millionaire thing was close at all. I should also add that by the time of marriage I had already played in a Christian rock band for two years and had also been a paid staff youth minister for over six years. So it would seem that the millionaire thing was next. But what, or should I say how, would this happen when we were so far in debt, with no hope this century of getting out.

If that last statement were true, I would have no reason to write a book. But the truth is that within three to three-and-a-half years of our marriage, we went from a huge negative net worth to a positive net worth, to all credit cards being paid off, to my wife with new credit and a much higher credit score, and to a beautiful new home, and this was just the start. How could this have happened? Each chapter in this book tells you of the steps we took to get out of debt and well on the road to being millionaires. These steps and ideas can be followed for your and your family's future. If you are looking to have lots of money *someday*, then you will need this book *today* because the odds are greater that those who receive large sums of money without applying these principles will become broke very quickly.

So why would I write this book? Arguments over finances are the number one reason for divorce in America. More Americans have record consumer debt then ever before. The average age of individuals with credit cards is growing younger everyday. Many teens, while still in high school, receive their first credit card. The number of active credit cards per person is also going up. So why would I write this book? Because there are growing numbers of people who fall into the death grip of debt like I did. I admit that part of my personality is that I like to help others. I enjoy doing things for others that benefit them. I am enjoying writing this book because I know it will help others. Also, I am moving beyond getting out of debt toward becoming a millionaire. The groundwork is already laid, and within about thirty more years I will be a millionaire without any more extra work. However, my efforts now (including this book, coming seminars, and other ongoing ventures) will shorten this period to only a few years. This goal will happen even if this book and the seminars don't work out, because they are not my only source of extra income. There are many others underway, and some will be started after this book is finished. So I write this book, not to become a millionaire overnight, but to motivate and encourage others to break the grip of debt around their necks, to break the chains holding them down from reaching their fullest potential, and to let others know that if I could do it then they can too.

This book is not about *getting rich quick* or about *ten easy ways to get out of debt*. Instead this book is designed to help you, among other things, to plug the leaks that have been draining your income. So many of my friends suffer from slow leaks within their budget process, but they can't see it. I can see it because I've been there, and I know what the leaks look like and how to stop them. This book will help you learn to plug the leaks by decreasing your spending, maximizing your earnings, and using the difference to pay off your debt and build savings. If I had relied on the earnings from my first job after being married to pay off all my debts, then I would still be in debt to this day. The aim is not to stop spending or to only buy cheaper products, but just to know when and what to buy and how this fits in with your overall goals.

My close friends call me anal when it comes to finances. And compared to them, I probably am. If you would call having a goal and a plan for my money anal, then I guess I am. However, in comparison to my friends who have no plan or reasonable expectations of where they will be financially in even five years, I really look obsessive. Most people have no idea. They go through their week doing their job and having some fun, they get paid, they pay bills, they go out on the town, and then they start all over again, all along wishing to have more money, hoping to hit the big lotto or get a call about the rich person who placed their name in a will. These hopes are in vain and only add to our overall misery and disappointment.

The theory of becoming a millionaire is easy. It's so easy that anyone can do it. However, few will ever attempt it. If you had taken one dollar per day since you started working, assuming the average person today starts working at age sixteen, and had placed the money in an account earning an average of 12.5 percent interest, then at age sixty-six you would have just under $1.2 million. Or, say starting at age twenty you place $2,000 or 10 percent of your income (whichever is greater) annually in a fund earning 14.5 percent interest for thirty years, you would be enjoying not less than $1 million at age fifty.

But, if you can't get your finances to the place where you can save $2,000 or 10 percent of your income, or even to the point that you care what percent it is making, then you will never have this to live on. The majority of people would love to be out of debt and to have much more money in their bank account. However, the same majority can't find their way out of debt, mostly because they don't understand how they got there in the first place. Getting out seems to be something they have even less knowledge about.

So what can you do? Good question. I suggest the following:

Do something!

Sounds a little simple, but in that simple statement lies the secret. Doing a little something is miles better than doing nothing. Doing something is going to get you out of debt years faster than doing nothing. Doing something will propel you to financial freedom and out of the slavery of debt. Start with studying this book. Okay, you don't like this book, or me? Fine, read someone else's book. Don't like to read? Then listen to an audio CD. Don't have the money to buy an audio CD? Then get a job and earn the money. If all you want to do is create excuses, then you are not really ready to get out of debt. Oh, you may want to get out of debt, but you surely are not ready. You make too many excuses and place the blame on someone or something else. Realize now that you are ultimately responsible for yourself. You, not the government, not family, not friends, nor anyone else is responsible.

You may feel that the cards you have been dealt in life are not fair, that life has given you an unfair hand to play and that you can't do it. Well, that is not true. Regardless of what your life has been and how far you are in debt to others, you can do it. There is a way out if you are ready. You need to just choose the why, and the how will follow. You can do this if the motivation is strong enough. Look deep within yourself and see the hopes and dreams that lie there. Look within to find out what motivates you. Then take action. Do something. Start today.

The sooner you start, the more you will have, both now and later. So, if you are serious about wanting to get started and understand that some things will be easy and that others will take hard work, then please read on. This book was meant for you. This book is short and easy to read, with lots of personal examples and real ways that you can succeed too.

2

Accomplishing 80 Percent of Your Goals Is Better than 100 Percent of Nothing

Chapter 2:
Accomplishing 80 Percent of Your Goals Is Better than 100 Percent of Nothing

Setting a goal is a way or form of measuring one's results. A goal is not a do-it-all-100-percent-or-you're-going-to-burn-in-hell type of thing. It is a measurement, a way for you to better yourself. Take archery, for example. What if you gave your child a bow-and-arrow set to play with in the backyard? After about an hour, you check on your child to make sure nothing has gone wrong. To your stunned amazement you find that there is a bull's-eye on the side of the shed and that your child has hit it right in the middle. You also notice that there is another one on the tree, on the house, on the fence, and on the neighbor's doghouse. All have an arrow right in the center of the bull's-eye. You get excited and ask if your child did this. "Yes!" is the response, exclaimed with the excitement of a child. "How did you hit the bull's-eye every time?" you ask. "It's easy. You first place the arrow in the bow and fire it, and then you go draw a bull's-eye around the arrow." Many people work their finances this way. They go out and work hard all year, and wherever they end up is where the bull's-eye is drawn. This kind of money management will lead to huge amounts of debt.

If I were to learn archery, my starting goals would be to hit the bull's-eye with one out of ten arrows from twenty-five feet away within one year. Say over the next year I practiced for one hour a day, four days a week. At the end of the year, what if I could hit the bull's-eye an average of once for every 12.5 arrows fired? That is hitting 80 percent of my goal. I would be so excited. At the start of the year, I did not know how to shoot any arrows, and now I'm hitting the bull's-eye with one out of every 12.5 arrows, on average. That's great! But wait, my goal was one out of ten. Why would I be happy for missing my goal? *Because my goal does not determine my happiness.* I am celebrating that I have gone from nothing to hitting the bull's-eye on a fairly good average. Now, the next year I would set a new goal. Maybe one out of five from thirty feet away. But for this year, I am happy.

The important thing to remember here is that goals are not life or death. They are set to give you a measurement to use on your way to your ultimate goal. Oh, by the way, notice that even though I did not achieve my first year's goal, the new year's goal was different and harder. Every year, new goals come around. Old goals go by the wayside. This is another reason not to get so lost in the feeling of missing your goal. Celebrate the victory of where you have come from and move on to the next goal.

Before I talk about the hows of what I did to get out of debt, let me take an important minute and talk about the why, for the why is much more important than the how. I have had this thought in my mind about being a millionaire for a very long time. Standing in my way of this reality was a huge mountain of debt and other credit problems unknown to me at the time. But it was not until after I was married that the why started to take shape. I saw that I had more in life to be responsible for. My wife and child were now more important to me than myself. The thoughts in my head turned to how their lives were going to be in five to ten years. What would happen to them if I were gone? How could I make sure they were taken care of if that were to happen? Also, my mother has reached a point in her life where her income is limited and her monthly expenses are not. I would love to be able to help her. There are other matters that are important to me also. I would love to do youth ministry at a church that cannot afford a paid staff youth minister. I would love to help more at the church I am currently attending. I would love to help out other ministries and ministers I know, and many I do not know yet. These are just a few of the things that now make up my why. The why, not the how, made the most difference to me.

You will now need to discover and write down these three things:

First: Why—The reason you are going to get out of debt.

Second: Your Goals—What you want to achieve.

Third: How—The daily, weekly, or monthly steps to achieving your goals.

Step One: Focus on your why. Gather pictures of your whys, like your wife, kids, and other motivating factors bigger than yourself. Make a collage and place it where you will see it every day and often throughout the day. As a matter of fact, go ahead and make two or more. Spread them around your office, car, home, and any other place you frequent. Every time you look at them, you will gain strength to persevere through the tough times and run faster in the good times.

I recommend staying away from the trap of placing things as your motivating factors. We may really want some very nice things, but they really don't motivate us, and they sure are not something bigger than ourselves. You want to look to something that will last beyond your time on earth, or that is very special while you are here. Make it specific, not just, "I want to be debt free." This is more in the lines of an outcome, not a goal. If you follow everything in this book, you will be debt free. But what is the reason you will do this? What will stop you from giving up when you are halfway through? You need a strong why. Don't pick a cheap and easy why. Make it special, honorable, and then strive mightily for it.

My personal whys are my wife, my two kids, my mother, church, other ministries, and creating a fund that will keep giving long after I am gone. These are my whys. I feel that my time here on earth is very limited, and I want to be spending more time on what counts than on things that fade, like my day job.

Step Two:

I must admit that I missed this step as I was first writing this book. However, this is the most important step. If you are married, you and your spouse must *both* be in agreement on your whys, your goals, and your budget. If one spouse is working hard to get both out of debt, and the other is working hard to keep them there, then many huge problems will come soon, not the least being a possible divorce.

In many ways, I have been blessed with a wonderful wife. When it came time for us to get out of debt and go for the life that we both wanted, she was right there with me. We both agreed and made the hard choices every day. Without this common goal, we would not have made it.

Now, on the other hand, if you are single, then this will be the easiest step for you, unless you are someone with multiple personalities. In that case, good luck and get help.

Step Three:

Set your goals. When you have step one done, step three will be easy because your goals (the things you would like to achieve) will flow right out of your why. For example, my goals would be to build a strong financial net for my wife and kids; to teach my kids about business, helping others, and God; to help my mother with her ever-increasing bills; to give money to missions; to fund new start-up churches; and so on. These goals flow right out of my personal why. So will yours.

At the beginning of each year, my wife and I take a night and set our goals for the year. Keeping in mind our overall why, we make a list with many different goals and discuss each one. If, after some discussion, we decide that a particular goal is not right, we simply scratch it off the list. My wife at first found this to be a stupid exercise, but because she loved me, it was one she endured. Well, our first year of marriage, we set our goals. Later that year, she wanted a family portrait. By the way, they are not cheap. So I told her that our goals had been set and that until we had extra money we would not be able to do a family portrait. This was a great excuse for something I really did not want to do anyway. So, came the new year, and our little goal-setting time. She said we should have a goal to get a family portrait. We discussed it. I personally had a problem with it because of the expense and the time it takes to get it done. Well, then I started to listen to her side and found a new understanding. The picture was not for my wife or me. It would truly be for our children years from now. But now a new problem came up. What about the rest of the time? I mean, what about the other events, vacations, and trips we take with them? Don't they want to remember these things, too, and show their kids? So not only did a family portrait become a goal, but also a family yearbook to help our kids remember all the great times we had.

So take a moment and start to think, "What would I like to achieve this year?" Think big. Think large. Write your ideas down. You might want to keep a piece of paper in your pocket all day so that when you have an idea for a goal you can write it down and make sure it gets on the master list. How long should your list be? That would be up to you. Mine is normally between twenty to thirty different goals.

Some of my friends have laughed and made fun of my yearly goal-making time and list of goals. They have said it will not make a difference and that it's just silly. Well, to them I say this each year, "On average my wife and I achieve 80 percent of our goals. How about you? I bet you hit 100 percent of your goals. Oh, but you have nothing as your goal. So I guess you succeed each and every year." They really have not understood what I have meant by that. But they do wonder how my wife and I have achieved so much in a short time. They look at the house we live in and the new cars we drive. They ask if these were our goals. I say, "No, these items are just the byproduct of our goals and our why." They still have no clue.

I suggest you write your goals down. Once will be enough. This will help clarify and organize your thoughts. I don't recommend you write them down daily or say them three times a day. That, to me, is just busywork, and time is too precious for me. Besides, if your why is big enough and the goals flow directly from that why, I bet you will never forget your goals or have any problem explaining them to anyone who asks, because it comes from your heart. No written paper can be more powerful than that.

Step Four:

This is the step before you create a budget. This is the how. Part of understanding how to get from point A to point B on a map is knowing where point A is. That is what we are going to do first. You need to understand where you are financially. Knowing all your assets and debts or liabilities is part of this process. As you compile these numbers, you might become a little depressed. But I hope instead that you will become more determined to pay them off and become debt free.

My wife and I were totally unaware of just how bad off we were. Our credit card debts totaled over $18,000, plus a car loan and a hospital bill. Our grand total was over $34,000 of debt. A family of three, we had no jobs and only one car; life was looking rough. But knowing where we started keeps us very appreciative of what we have. Just a few short years ago we had nothing. We were able to see our progress as we climbed out of debt. This progress was not evident every month. But every four to six months I would sit down with my wife and show her how our progress was going. This helped us both see that there was an end to the tunnel and that we were on our way.

Now is the time for the how. Actually, the majority of this book is about the how, including the first two steps, but let's keep this simple. Draw a line in the sand of your situation and say, "This is it; no more debt." There are two ways to do this. First, you can do it yourself. (You can use the form that comes with this book, called THE LINE IN THE SAND.) Make a list of all your regular ongoing bills, how much you owe to creditors, how much you make, and how much you have in assets. Second, you can go to a financial adviser and have them help you do a financial-needs analysis. They will ask you for all this information, organize it, and place it on nice charts. They may or may not charge you for this, so make sure you ask. If they don't charge you a fee, they might be looking to sell you something. Make sure they understand that you are looking to get out of debt first and then invest. If they are smart, they will stay in touch, because one day you will need someone to help you choose the right investments—more about that in the next book.

However you get this done does not matter. The importance lies in *getting it done*. Keep this report handy at all times while going through this book. I will refer back to it often. As you make new goals, you will want to remind yourself where you started and notice how far you have come. This will be a great source of encouragement to you. Remember that even if you hit 80 percent of your first year's goal of getting out of debt, it is much better than hitting 100 percent of no goal at all!

3

*Stop Spending More than You
Make!*

Chapter 3:
Stop Spending More than You Make!

Take a look now at your line in the sand. If you are like most people, you are spending more than you make. Look for yourself and see. Are you spending more than you have coming in? Author Robert Allen, in his book *Multiple Streams of Income*, tells of his "bathtub theory of economics." It goes like this (paraphrased to the best of my ability). Money flows into your money bathtub through money faucets. Money flows out of your money bathtub through leaks or drains at the bottom of the tub. Most people think the way to get rich is to turn on more faucets. That is not right. You need to plug the leaks at the bottom before the bathtub will begin to overflow. After that is done, turning on more faucets will only increase the speed at which you become rich.

If you are spending more than you make, you have too many holes in your bathtub. No matter how much you make, money will always flow out at a high rate of speed. This is why many instant millionaires become broke within five years of receiving the money. They never stopped the leaks. So we are going to look at ways of plugging the holes. First we will look to cut out spending and/or change how we spend. As for myself, I had to do both. When my wife and I sat down and went over our budget, we had way too many holes in our bathtub. So we started to make some hard decisions because our desire was to get out of debt. Following are some of the decisions we made.

We canceled our cable service (this saved about thirty-five dollars a month) and replaced it by purchasing an antenna for the television for forty dollars. So, the next month we started saving thirty-five dollars each month.

My wife is from Indiana, and we were living in Florida at the time. So having no long distance phone service was not an option. One night my mother-in-law was telling me how she has this great long-distance plan and only pays four cents a minute. We were paying a whole lot more than that, so I asked her how she did it. She asked me if I had ever received a call from another long-distance phone company. I said, "Yes, all the time." I tell them no and to please stop calling. "Wrong move," she said. "You should talk with them and keep track of what rates they give you. You might be surprised." Well sure enough, within a month my long-distance bills were cut by 60 percent or more. My brother has a different way that he has shared with me. His idea is to cancel long-distance coverage on your house phone, because even if you don't place long-distance calls they still charge you to have the service available. To replace this he purchases a phone card from Sam's Club and uses it as his service to make toll calls. I took this idea and applied it to my cell phone. For me the best rate plan for my cell phone (which I have because of my work) was to have an unlimited plan with local calls only. For my toll calls, I use the phone card.

Here is a short list of ways to save or cut expenses.

Turn up the thermostat or turn off the A/C during summer.
Schedule an appointment with your power company to get suggestions on other ways to save.
Disconnect cable TV or limit it to the bare basics (five to seven channels).
Don't eat out. Take your lunch to work.
Plan your dinner meals for the week. Go to the grocery store only one time per week.
Make a list before going into any store and stick to that list.
Buy in bulk—compare first, don't assume the savings.
What you buy, buy on sale (sodas, meats, other food items, etc.)
Cut out long-distance phone calls. Shop for a better rate plan.
For car—or homeowners insurance, call five different places for quotes.
Never use cash—use a bank Visa check card instead (more on this later).
Stop using your charge cards, except for emergencies (flat tire, car repair, etc.)
Cancel expensive Internet service and go to a free service or one that is less than ten dollars a month.
Volunteer to help out the needy/homeless/poor.
Stop change spending (on gum, crackers, snacks, sodas, etc.)
If you drink or smoke, cut back.
Consolidate credit card bills. Try to move the balances to as few cards as possible.
Install a timer on the hot-water heater in your home.
Cut out nonessential reoccurring bills (newspapers, magazines, subscriptions, etc.)
Save all the savings.
(There are a few Web site resources listed in the back of this book that you might find helpful in your fight to get out of debt.)

The most expensive hamburgers I have ever eaten are the ones for which I pay *cash*. Over the last six years, I have carried paper money very few times. I use that wonderful little invention called the Visa check card (or MasterCard check card, depending on your bank). Everywhere I purchase something, that card is how I pay. It works like a charge card and comes right out of my checking account. I save a lot of money this way, too. How, you might ask? Good question. To answer, I need to tell you about the day I discovered that I had just eaten a twenty-dollar hamburger. One day I was in a rush to leave and failed to pack a lunch. So I though I would just come home at noon and make my sandwich. Well, many unscheduled things happened that morning, and I was not able to get home because of a scheduled appointment. I stopped by the local ATM of my bank and pulled out twenty dollars in cash. This is the smallest amount you can pull out using the ATM. So I went to a drive-through and ordered a hamburger. This was on a Monday. By Friday, my wife asked me if I had two dollars. Our child needed to purchase some supplies from her school for a project she was working on. I thought, "Sure, I just picked up cash on Monday." I opened my wallet, and there was nothing, not a single dollar bill. I stopped to think what had happened in five days that I would have spent twenty dollars. At first I could not remember a thing. Then I slowly started to remember that there was the dollar I spent at work on a candy bar, the dollar for the soda out of the machine, and so on, all week. I could not believe it at the time. I had spent the whole twenty dollars—all on little junk stuff, nothing of substance, just thrown away on impulse items. Twenty dollars was gone because of a stupid hamburger. And so I have learned to never carry cash. If I have it, I will spend it and not know where it went. I use the check card, and that way I have to record each transaction in the checkbook. This also reminds me where I am spending my money. If I need to have lunch, I now go to a place that will take the card. Even if I have to pay a small fee for the service, for me it is far better then spending twenty dollars on one hamburger.

Volunteer to help out the needy/homeless/poor. This might sound like a strange way to save money, but let me explain. One summer when I was a youth pastor, I took about fifteen students on a trip to Mexico and then to a youth convention in San Antonio, Texas. For seven days we were surrounded by the poorest of the poor—not like here in America, but people who slept on the floor of their house made out of dirt (not just the floor was dirt, but the house itself was made of dirt). Their bathroom (if they were lucky) was a hole dug in the ground, with sheets hung around for some privacy. This was a very poor place. Then, at the end of seven days, we found our little group in a multimillion-dollar hotel in downtown San Antonio. This was a huge contrast to where we had been that morning. We talked about this difference for the rest of our time in Texas. The kids and I definitely changed our perspective on money and things. What is necessary and what truly is not? The difference between our wants, needs, and desires is huge, and that trip made it very easy to see. If you have a problem giving up something like cable TV for a short time until you get out of debt, my suggestion would be to go help out your local homeless shelter, battered mother's shelter, or teen crisis center. You will truly find out just how good you have it in life compared to others who are truly in a terrible situation. A girl just came to our church this past weekend. Her last surviving parent just passed away. She is nineteen and orphaned. With that said, how difficult will it be to give up cable for a year to a year and a half?

Whether you believe in God, religion, or other higher power, you will find great perspective in helping those less fortunate than you. You will gain more appreciation for the good things in your life. You will find that you take care of things better but at the same time do not get upset about them.

I went back to Mexico again with a friend's youth group from his church the following summer. I met them in Mobile, Alabama. I parked my car in a church parking lot and boarded their van for the ride down. It was another great trip. I was looking for the lesson of this trip that would stand out like the last. Everything was great. We accomplished a lot while we were down there. Many of the locals I had met the previous year were there and remembered me. Things could not have been better. So the time came to go home. I boarded the van with my friends, and they drove me back to our meeting point in Alabama. It was Sunday morning and the church was in service when we pulled into their parking lot. Our van drove right past the place where I had parked my car. The only problem was that there was a blue car there, and mine was white. We drove a lap around the parking lot with my friend asking, "Are you sure you parked it there?" We stopped, and I said, "My car is gone." My friend hopped out and went to ask the church if for some reason they had towed my car. They told us they had not and that the car had been missing for about three days. They thought I had come back early and had gone home. Needless to say, my friends were a little freaked out. However, I was calm and hardly phased by this. We called the police, and I filled out a report. I received a call three days later informing me that the police had found my car, or what was left of it. Still I was not really affected by this event. I figured that if this was the worst thing happening to me, a temporary inconvenience, then that was great. The people I had met in Mexico had many more problems to deal with than the loss of a car.

This story goes on just a little more. I needed to buy a new car (one that ran would be nice). So I went to the car lot where a friend at my church worked. I purchased a new car that day. I was very excited. This was my first-ever brand new car. When I got in for a test drive, there were only 2.5 miles on the odometer. Within one week of owning the car, one of my students opened the car door hard and hit the large vehicle parked next to me. This placed a nice crease and dent in my door, and of course did nothing to the other vehicle. The student cringed with a look of terror, fearful that I would yell or scream. But instead I simply shrugged it off and said something sarcastic like, "I think now you owe the car an apology and should see if it would like a Band-Aid." This really surprised the student, and myself. Later that night I thought about the event and why I did not get upset. I believe I had a shift in my thoughts about things that I own. I want to take care of them better, but I am not going to let my things own me and control the way I feel or react. This attitude has helped me often along the way of getting out of debt. I had to cut many things out of my life to save money and get my budget in line, but they were just things. A temporary cut. Nothing permanent. So why would I get upset about losing cable for a year?

One of our friends asked us how we got out of debt so fast. We started to answer by listing some of the things we had stopped spending money on. Immediately her response was, "I could never do that. I would just die without cable." Her response was so horrible that you would have thought we had just told her to cut off her right hand. Now that would be bad. But cable TV is just a thing. I'm not really home all that much anyway. Why get so upset over a thing? Now I have cable again. I value it, I like it, and I'm glad we have it again. Could I live without it again? Sure, no problem. There are more important things in life than cable TV, like all my whys. So if you find that you are having a hard time giving something up, then help out those who are truly in need and have very little.

Plan your dinner meals for the week; go to the grocery store only one time per week. I must admit that I have a wonderful wife. On top of all the numerous wonderful traits about her, she is also a great cook. This skill carried us through the tough times. She would plan our dinners for the week on Saturday and would then go to the store to purchase all she needed. I was amazed at what she could do and how our per-meal cost was averaging about six dollars. And that fed all three of us. For example, beef would be the first meal, and the next night there was beef quesadilla. Then we had chicken, and the next night chicken Caesar salad. We rarely had leftovers. She always cooked more than we needed for one meal and just found another way to prepare what was left for the next night. At each meal we had vegetables or a salad, of course, but the main expense is the meat. She would locate the good sales or would purchase in bulk what we needed for the week, and we were able to get by on very little. This was a good thing because in the early days of our marriage we had just that—very little!

If you are not currently tracking how much you spend on food at home and you per-meal cost, take a week or a month and track what you spend. Find an average per-meal cost and plan a way to get the cost down without living on little square packaged bricks of noodles.

Save all the savings. My oldest brother stopped smoking a few years back. When he told me this, I was shocked and amazed. His habit had gotten up to three packs a day. Each week he spent a lot of money on cigarettes, so when he quit I asked what he was going to do with the money he was saving. He said that each week he was going to place the amount of money he would have spent on cigarettes in a jar, and at the end of summer his family was going on a trip. They had a nice trip, with nothing more than saving the savings.

There is a huge lesson for all of us here. The point of all these saving suggestions is that you can put the money you save toward your debt, or start living within your income, not so you can take a vacation or buy those new shoes you have been wanting. Our why is set, and we need to stay with that until it is accomplished. The shoes will come, and that vacation will happen, just not today. Give it some time. Remember to stay focused. One of my bosses would say it this way: "Plan your work and then work your plan."

4

Here's the Secret: 10 Percent, 10 Percent, and 80 Percent

Chapter 4:
Here's the Secret: 10 Percent, 10 Percent, and 80 Percent

In your line-in-the-sand analysis, have you given 10 percent of your income away to charity? Have you paid yourself next with 10 percent of your income? Make sure you calculate these figures from your gross pay and not your net. The gross pay is the total dollars you have earned before taxes, 401(k), insurance, and other items that are normally deducted from our paychecks. There should be a line on your pay stub marked GROSS EARNINGS. Locate this line and multiply the number by .10 on a calculator to figure 10 percent. After you have deposited your paycheck into your bank, write the checks—one to your church or charity, and another to yourself. Deposit the one to yourself into a *separate* savings account. *Do not* leave this money in your checking account.

When my wife and I first started, we did not have any extra money. Every dime was needed to pay our bills, and we were still short. But we always took the 10 percent out for our donation. This was very important to us, and we did it with every paycheck. Aside from the faith aspect of our giving, this was still very important to us. We understand that there are others in our own town and across this land who are in worse situations then we are. We do not want to become so fixed on ourselves that we forget about others. As we look toward others' situations, we find out just how good we really have it and develop a larger appreciation for the few things that we do have.

As you calculate your 10 percent to charity, 10 percent to yourself, and then your bills, does this figure balance with what your line in the sand says you need to have? If not, go back to chapter 3 and find some more leaks to plug. I had to keep going back many times to find areas to cut out or cut back. Mostly we cut out spending because we were so far over our income, but every payday the first check I would write would be for my 10 percent to charity. This never seemed to make sense, giving money away when it seemed we did not have enough for ourselves. But at the end of each month, all bills were paid, and so was the tithe.

I should let you know that if the discussion about God makes you nervous or angers you, you should please go on to the next half of this chapter, called "10 Percent for Me." Don't bother reading on, for you will only find what you don't like.

I know these things to be true. Tithing is not what we do for God, but it is what God does for us. I give out of love and reverent respect and reverent fear, not because I expect something in return. I give to give, not to get, for what more of a blessing can God give me than his Son and the total forgiveness of my sins? Giving is a daily reminder that God, not my paycheck, is first in my life. I serve my Father, not my job. I celebrate the 90 percent of my paycheck he gives me, for I have my job and my life because of him. My family comes from him. All that I have and all that I am comes from him, and all he asks is 10 percent back to show respect. It is a very small price to pay and a large offering of respect to the God I love.

I have gotten very upset when I have heard some pastors talk about money and tithing. Some have said that if you give, God will give you back tenfold. If you tithe $100, he will give you $1,000, and if you tithe $100,000, he will give you $1 million. They say this comes from the Bible. Well, I have read the Bible more than twice, and I have not found that to be true. I have found where he promises that if we give our tithe to him, he will overfill our storehouses, but does that mean with money? No, it does not. Again I say, what more of a blessing can God give us than his Son and the total forgiveness of our sins? Many pastors have used money as a controlling, binding, enslaving, and manipulating thing with their congregations. Shame on them. God still loves them, but shame on them for placing chains on those whom Christ has set free.

I have met many people in churches who get upset when it comes to the discussion of money and God. They think it is no one's business but their own and that everyone has to give what they feel God is telling them to give. Well I say shame on you, too. If you get that upset at the discussion of money, you might want to look at what is most important in your life. If God is on the throne, you would not be that upset. But when we put money on the throne, then we will be upset and get angry.

The first argument (for lack of a better term) that my wife and I had was over tithing. She had always given from the gross dollar amount of her paycheck. I, however, took my giving from the net figure. So we talked about this for a couple of nights. Then I realized just what we were really arguing about. It came down to about three dollars and some change. I started to laugh because it seemed so silly to be in disagreement with my wife over three dollars and some change. So I told her I would agree with her, and from then on we calculated our giving from the gross wages earned each payday.

I can tell you that when I did my line in the sand and the first budget for my wife and I over six years ago, the money we brought in was way less than what went out. But we were faithful, and we tithed. We might not have saved 10 percent for ourselves, but we tithed every payday, no matter how the finances looked. At the end of every month, the bills were paid, and we survived. How did this happen? Only two answers come to mind: "I don't know" and God. That's it. Nothing else explains it. My wife and I often look back at our situation and shake our heads in amazement, but those two answers are the only ones that come to mind. However, only the last one do we truly believe.

10 Percent for Me

The second 10 percent is for you. Learn to pay yourself before any other bills. So many people go through life working for someone else and never pay themselves from what they earn. If you don't believe me, just ask yourself, how much money do you have that you paid yourself from three years ago? For most people the answer would be *zero*. Why do we work so hard and stress out so much over our jobs and not take a small percentage for ourselves out of our paycheck? This simple fact of paying yourself first can have a huge impact on how well you live at the age of sixty-five. For example, if you started at eighteen years old with a job paying six dollars an hour, you stayed at that job until you were sixty-five and ready for retirement, you never received any bonuses or pay increases, you never got a 401(k) plan or stock options, and when you retired all you received was a slice of cake, what would you have if you paid yourself 10 percent before any bills? You are probably thinking, "Not much," and that there is no way you would stay in a nonpaying, nonpromoting job like that for all those years. But if you did you would have $1,300,000 to retire on.

Now you say, "That sounds nice, but I must have placed an unusually high interest rate on that or something." Nope! You just place that amount away from your touch, earning 10 percent interest per year, and place 10 percent of your income in that account every year, year in and year out, never missing, but always placing that 10 percent away for the day that is coming quick. But how do you get a 10 percent interest rate on your money when your bank is only offering 2 percent at best for a savings account? I would not place my very long-term money there. I would find a good mutual fund that was earning at least 10 percent in a bad year and go with that one. Oh, by the way, just in case you could find a mutual fund that earned about 15 percent interest for all those years, you would have $7,600,000 at your retirement, or you could stop working after age fifty-one with just over a million dollars. That's fourteen years earlier. Now are you starting to see the importance of paying yourself before any other bills and right after your tithe? This is important to your whys!

For my wife and I, this was the hardest to do. We owed so much. How could we save money? Our thought was to place this "paying ourselves" money toward our bills. We went back and forth on this. Overall, we paid ourselves about 5 percent of our total income. This came in the form of my wife's 401(k) plan that her employer offered. We had them take out 10 percent of her pay toward this plan. They also matched 50 percent of what we placed in the fund. That was awesome! We compromised with this amount of savings until we were out of debt. If I could go back, I would have taken 10 percent out of my paycheck for savings also.

This money every payday just started to add up. At the end of the first year we had a small amount in the account. We were both pleased with our progress. The next year we were flat stunned into silence. Not only did the money we placed in there the first year compound interest, but then the next year's money went on top of that, and Wow, what a difference. The end of the third year was even better. This is when I started kicking myself for not taking the 10 percent from my paycheck every week and putting it away. The little bit from her check plus the interest and the company's matching funds made for a huge amount to us.

If your company has an automatic deduction plan (savings, 401(k), retirement, stocks, etc.), make sure you sign up and have them take 10 percent out each payday. If you think you are too far in debt and that 10 percent would be too much, have them take out 5 percent instead. The point here is to get started, and started right away. The same goes for your spouse if you have one.

If your company does not offer automatic deductions, you will have to be strong. Set up a savings account so that you would have to go into the bank to access the money. Make the money hard but not impossible to get to. Have a plan to make deposits every payday into this account. Do it by dropping the deposit off at the bank or by mailing the deposit to them. Now comes the hard part. You must actually do this each paycheck. You will not find that overnight you have a huge amount in the bank, but over time this will add up. Continue to do this for ten to twelve months. At that time, find a mutual fund company that will allow you to invest in small amounts. Open an account and send your 10 percent each payday to the mutual fund. The money in the savings account will be your emergency reserve in case some huge event happens that you need money for, like losing your job or a major sickness. The bank will pay very little in interest, but something is better than nothing. The mutual fund will pay more in interest and should be considered your very long-term investment. Do not touch this account. Please contact a financial advisor for more information about what fund would be right for you.

In short, the theory here is to give the first 10 percent of your income away toward helping others. The benefits are enormous no matter how you look at it. Just the tax deductions alone will help you in the long run. Don't skip this first

10 percent. The next 10 percent goes to you. This is to start your long-term savings and wealth. Start today with as much as you can. The 80 percent left is what you will have to live on. Pay all your bills and buy things you may want, need, or desire. A person who can live within this formula for their working life will be very wealthy come retirement and will help many people and organizations along the way.

So, if the 10-10-80 rule is the secret, why don't more people know about it? It's because we, as a society, desire things like having it our way, right now, without any regards to affordability. Why are there four convenience stores within a quarter mile of my house? Because people in my neighborhood don't want to drive five miles to the grocery store? No, because there are also three large grocery stores and a huge department store all in that same quarter mile. People want the convenience of the quick-in store. They will pay a little more to save one block of driving. It becomes a real shame when minute rice takes too long. When you can't wait to microwave your dinner, you go to a drive-through to pick something up. Many will cry foul when the price of gas goes up five cents a gallon. However, when you think about it, your tank only holds fifteen gallons of gas, so that is an extra seventy-five cents per fill-up. And these same people who cry over the price of gas will walk right into the convenience store where they filled up and pay a dollar more for a gallon of milk than if they had gone to the grocery store one block down the road. How does this make sense? What a waste of time all of that is—that one block saved, not waiting on dinner but waiting on a drive-through, griping about gas prices while paying a dollar more for milk. All this becomes expensive when you figure out how long you have to work for that. Think before you spend. Take the extra time to walk a little more. Save the extra money.

5

A Few Words on Budgets

Chapter 5:
A Few Words on Budgets

This is the dreaded word. Budget. Not many people like budgets. They have found them hard to stick to, and they are unhappy when they do stay on budget. Many people have this same thought about diets, but a good diet is the most effective way to lose weight. Likewise, a good budget will help you lose your unwanted debt. Diets also, like budgets, after the desired results have been achieved, allow you to relax the restrictions and develop a lifestyle for you to live with that is much more enjoyable. Remember that you are at your worst financial place right now. Better financial days are just ahead. Just make it through a few tough days, and then the sun will shine again.

A restrictive budget will be hard to live by. But how long do you really need to live by this restrictive budget? Only a short period of time in comparison to the life you will live after you are out of debt. This is very true.

The tighter the budget you have, the quicker you will get out of debt, and the more motivated you will be to get out of debt quickly.

A budget is like a tool someone would use to get a specific job done. As with most jobs, you may need many different tools. The same is true of your finances and budgets. You will need to reevaluate your budget many times along the way. At each step, you will find that you can move resources here and relax restrictions slightly over there. This will happen as your bills are paid down and your income increases. So don't fear this step. Put a lot of thought into your budget. This is the tool you will be using to lose your debt weight.

There are many different budget worksheets you can choose from. Most home computers come with a budget worksheet template as part of the basic package. Look for one you like or simply make up one of your own. I made up my own and have included a sample in this book. On the left side of the paper I have listed all my bills and payments. Then I have at least six columns to the right. The first is to carry any positive balances over from the month before. The next column is for my first pay date in the month and the bills I paid. The next column is for notes. The second-to-last column is for my last pay date in the month and the bills I paid from that check. The last column is for comments and to bring out balances and totals that need to be carried over to the next month.

The important idea here is to have a budget worksheet.

When people think about their finances and where the money goes, most can't tell you what they spent their money on. This is where we get in trouble. We have a false feeling that we still have money, so we spend more and more and more until we find ourselves so far in debt that we can't see a way out. Don't fall into this trap. Use the budget to help you know what you are spending your money on. Use the budget to guide and control your spending choices. Budgets don't tell you that you *can't* buy something you really want, just *when* you can afford it. So listen to your budget and make your purchases when they make sense.

Tracking where and what you spend your money on will help you stay on goal.

I stopped using cash a long time ago for almost all things. I have found another benefit from this. With using my Visa check card for all my purchases, I have to hold on to the receipt to record it in my checkbook. This is very important so that you don't start bouncing checks. That would be very bad. So, I have found that when I record my receipts, I start to notice a trend as to where specifically I spend my money. Some weeks I notice that we have spent a large amount at Wal-Mart. My wife and I talk, and we curb our spending for the next pay period. We have a regular amount we spend on food. Occasionally I will notice that we have more in grocery receipts than we should. After talking with my wife, I find out there was a great sale on beef and that she stocked up and placed lots in our freezer, and we won't have to buy any next week. Noticing the trends of your spending is very important. Doing something about them is even more important. If my brother picked up a hammer and started pounding my hand with it, it would be important to know that this hurts. However, it would be more important to do something about having him stop. That is my point. If something is going wrong, you will start to notice it, and you can make a correction as you are going through your month. I find this a great reason to use a Visa check card. If you do not have one, go this week to your bank and get one. If they say no, go to another bank. Find one that will say yes. There are lots of banks out there, and one will help you.

Expect the Unexpected

Many people find that budgets don't work because life happens. The car battery dies, or the tire goes flat. How about if your refrigerator stops working? This is all part of life. The problem is that most people make their budgets without putting in a space for life to happen. They fail to plan for the expected unexpected. Everyone will have these and more problems happen in their lives, so it is not a matter of *if* they will happen, but *when* they will happen. Learn to plan and expect the unexpected. This way you will be ready and prepared for what will come. So, in your budget worksheet, plan for unexpected life. For example, your budget has a line for car payment. Each week, when you take out money for your car payment, also take out two dollars more. Why? You will one day need to get new tires, fix a flat, get an oil change, or many other things that can go wrong with a car. Use this little bit to take the edge off the hit to your budget when it comes. You might not have all of it in there when the tire blows out, but if you have saved twenty dollars, and a new tire is sixty dollars, then all you have to come up with is forty dollars. Now that helps your budget continue working. There are a few items in my personal budget that I add money to for *life to happen*. They are my car, my house (payments and repairs), and my family. Over time this will start to add up. Also, as your budget gets better you will be able to add more and more money to these items.

Budgets are important, so don't delay in making yours. Every day you wait is only hurting you and your family. Here is where you need to remember your why. Why we do things is very important. This why helps us to do things that may not be enjoyable but are beneficial. Do it today. Don't put it off. Don't let procrastination and fear win this day from you.

6

Pay off Your Credit Cards, Then Cancel with Enthusiasm!

Chapter 6:
Pay off Your Credit Cards, Then Cancel with Enthusiasm!

Lets talk about credit cards and how to get rid of that debt. I have already mentioned that you will want to look at the possibility of transferring balances to other cards so that you are working with the fewest payments possible. You do *not* want to do this if you are trading to a higher-interest card than the one you currently have or if the card you are transferring a balance to charges a fee to do so. Many checks I receive in the mail from my credit cards to trade balances have a fee attached with them in fine print. However, I have found that some companies will offer no-fee transfers if you call and talk with a customer-service representative, who can tell you what, if any, fees there are.

After you have the fewest possible credit cards with balances, organize them in order of interest rate charged. On your budget worksheet, make sure the card with the highest interest is highlighted. This is the card you will be paying off first. To the other cards you will just pay the minimum payments.

So how do you pay off the high-interest card first? (Part 1)

Well, if you were lucky enough after making your cuts to be under budget, then apply the money you saved to the card. If not, then the next several chapters will cover how I was able to pay off my cards in record time.

My wife and I worked so hard to pay off that first credit card. It seemed like it took forever. I remember near the end I wrote a check for all but ten dollars. Time ticked slowly until the next billing cycle came in the mail. Then the final check was written. My wife and I celebrated. But then I waited until the next statement came in the mail. It was official: no balance due. I was so excited that I could not contain the joy I felt. I went inside the house and called the company on the phone. It was time to cancel my card. I was so very excited. The customer-service representative came on the phone and asked how she could help me. With great enthusiasm I said, "I'm calling to cancel my card." I was so happy at the time that I might have even laughed when I said that. The lady said she was sad to hear that and that she would like to know why I would be interested in canceling their card. I told her that for the past year my wife and I had been working hard to get out of debt and that this credit card company had the highest interest rate and was the first to be paid off. I explained that our goal was to pay off all debt and in the end keep only one or two cards that had the lowest interest. I told her I had received the statement in the mail showing a zero balance and that I was ready to cancel my card. All this was said with honest enthusiasm, mostly because I was definitely excited. This was a huge goal, and we were there! The lady again said she was sad to hear that I wanted to cancel, but wondered if there was anything they could do to keep my business. I had no idea what she meant, so I just restated our goals.

"We are paying off our entire debt one at a time. At the end, we will be keeping only one or maybe two cards that have the lowest interest. Your card had the highest rate, and you are the first one to be paid off."

The lady said, "So you have other cards with balances?"

"Yes," I said.

"You could transfer the balances from your other cards to this account," she said.

"But your company has the highest interest rate," I said.

After a few moments on hold, the lady informed me of a special they were having. I could transfer any other balances to them, and the interest rate would be 12 percent. This was a far cry from the 21 percent I had started with. I asked if there was a fee to do this. She said no. I asked if there was any other cost to doing it. Again she said no. So after about two seconds of thinking, I said yes. I ran to get my other credit card information with the next highest interest rate (18 percent). The credit limit was enough to transfer all but about $400 to the new formally paid-off card. This step saved me a lot of money in interest payments!

After three more months, I was able to pay off the remaining balance on the now highest-interest card. After I received the statement showing a zero balance, I called them up. With much enthusiasm I told them I was requesting to cancel my card and the reason why. They said okay and canceled my card on the spot. I must admit that after I got off the phone I was a little less excited. I was expecting them to offer me a better interest rate like the other company did. By the time my wife got home from work, my enthusiasm was back, and we cut the old credit card up. What a great moment that was. We went out to dinner to celebrate our victory. Just four more to go and we would be done.

Each credit card I canceled was different from the others. Just stay firm to what you want and don't give in. Hold out for the lowest possible fixed rate. Don't let them sidetrack you with any other offers or benefits they may have. You are looking for low interest rates and no annual fees for having the card. All others will be canceled. Keep only the two lowest-interest cards at the end. Cut up all others. Make sure you cancel them. Pull your credit report one to two times a year to make sure they have canceled your credit line. If they did not, it will affect your credit score later on.

On each credit card's last statement I would write the time, date, and person I talked to about canceling the card. One company told me they would cancel my card. Twelve months or so passed, and in the mail I received some convenience checks for the card that was canceled. I called the company and asked them what the checks were for. They told me they were to access my credit and could be used for anything I wanted. I asked them what credit. They said it was credit attached to my account. I asked them what account. They said my credit card account. "Is this account still active?" I asked. They said it showed the account was closed but was still in their system "in case I wanted to change my mind." Well, needless to say, I hit the roof. I yelled at that lady, and then I yelled at her boss. I was so steamed. I told them that if I *ever* received a statement, check, or card from them in reference to that account again, there was going to be huge trouble, which would be started with a letter from my lawyer. Needless to say I have never heard or received anything from that company again.

So how do you pay off the high-interest card first? (Part 2)

If you were not lucky enough to have extra money from your budget, this becomes harder. I said harder, not impossible. I did not have money left over at the end of my budget, and I am out of debt. So it can be done. There is just a little more work that needs to be done. And in those words lies the key.

A Little More Hard Work.

In the following chapters, I will tell you about many different ways my wife and I put in a little more hard work. Some, I must admit, was not even that hard. It was just a little more work. The major thought to keep in mind is that this hard work is only temporary. It is not permanent. Your debt will be paid off, you will be living within your budget and saving 10 percent, and there will be no more reason to have extra work. That sounds nice. A nice life without the headache of loads of debt hanging over your head. Nice!

7

Trading Up Your Job

Chapter 7:
Trading Up Your Job

So how were we able to pay off that first credit card so fast? Well, there were several techniques we used. In this chapter, I will tell you about *trading up your job*. Late one night, my wife and I were talking about her job. Okay, I was listening, and she was complaining. She had long since grown tired of the job and the hassles that came along with it. For the money, it was not worth the hassles. However, my wife is not one who likes to quit a job and struggle looking for a new one. By the end of our conversation, she was going to start looking for a new job. Not quitting her current job until she had a new employer was very important for us. I searched the Internet, and we started asking friends, looking for customer-service job openings for her. A couple of weeks went by, and then she found a good lead. She went through the application, resume, and interview processes. They liked her abilities, and she liked the company. My wife was making nine dollars an hour at the job she was unhappy in. The new company offered to start her out at thirteen dollars an hour. That was a huge increase for us. She would be doing the same type of work and have an increase of four dollars an hour, and more availability of overtime at time-and-a-half pay. SWEET! So after discussing it, she went into her current job and turned in her two-week notice. She served her two-week notice, and the following Monday she started her new job. The old job, however, asked her if she could stay on part-time to help clean up the backlog of work. This created two new problems and two new opportunities. The problem was *when* she could do this, and the opportunity was *how much* she would get paid. She told her old boss that she would be available a couple of hours each night at seventeen dollars an hour. This sounded outrageous to them. My wife explained that she was able to gain a couple of hours each night at her new job, and overtime at time and a half came to $19.50 an hour. So, in short, she would be losing money by coming back to her old job to work part-time. The management at that time did not agree to this amount, so my wife did not go back there to work. Shortly after that, there was a management change within the old company. They asked if my wife could come back part-time to help out. They approved her request for seventeen dollars an hour. They wanted her back. She went back to help out on a part-time basis. This lasted for about three weeks. Around the end of that time, the new management at the old job offered her old job back at a new salary position of $35,000 a year. This was a great offer. We talked, and she decided to go back. Now at this point we were just loving life. The increase in her pay was huge so far. How could it get any better? Well, she went to her new employer to tell them of her decision to go back to her old job and that the reason was because of a huge pay raise. Within three days the new employer countered with an hourly wage of fifteen dollars an hour and showed her that if she worked just one hour of overtime a day, she would be making $37,000 a year. Also, there was availability for even more overtime if she wanted. This was it. She gave a firm no thanks to the old boss and a permanent hello to the new boss. In a matter of one month, she went from nine dollars an hour to making almost double that. SWEET!!!

Many truths came out of this experience.

Truth #1: If an employer can keep an employee at nine dollars an hour, then why would they pay that person sixteen dollars an hour? There was no reason or motivation for my wife's old boss to pay her more—until she had another job that was willing to pay her more. Then the money gates opened wide.

Truth #2: Check the market about every two to three years to see what your worth is to other companies. You might be surprised. Even if nothing else had happened with her old boss, my wife still would have ended up making an increase of more then three dollars an hour. That's $120 a week and $480 a month. Now that much of an increase per month could help get anyone out of debt faster.

So now it is your turn. You have a job, and you want to see if you can trade up. The first thing to do would be to create a resume or update your old one. If you are not sure how to do this or you are unhappy with what you have, then may I suggest asking a friend? My wife had a friend who specialized in resume enhancement. This was a fancy title that meant she took an average word description and created multiword, upwardly sounding objectives and inserted them into your resume. I must admit she did a great job. If you do not have a friend to help, you can find these services in your local yellow pages. You want to spend time and, yes, some money (within reason) on having a great resume.

Next we want to work on our first impressions. Make sure you have sharp, coordinating, business-appropriate attire to wear when you go to fill out applications. Also make sure you have a second outfit for the follow-up interview. Are you worried that the new employer may contact your current boss? Let them know you do not want your current employer contacted because you have not told them you are looking.

Now you are ready to start looking. Where do you look? Start in your own field, or try something new. It does not matter. I used the Internet classifieds and the newspapers. I also walked into places where I thought I would like to work. There was no sign up, but I thought there was no harm in asking. I was right, too. My wife used an agency to help her find her new job. You could look for help-wanted signs in windows. Ask your friends if they know of any place hiring. You never know where the right job might be found.

What Do You Have to Lose?

My wife was scared about starting to look for another job. I remember many evening dinner conversations about "what if this" and "what if that." I told her, "What do you have to lose? If they say no, you still have your current job. If they say yes, but with less money, then you still have your current job. The absolute worst thing that can happen to you is that they offer you a job making more money. You can't lose, and you have everything to gain."

That is the truth. You have nothing to lose and everything to gain. There is no reason to feel scared, because this activity cost you nothing but time and a little effort. The company you apply to will know that you have a job and that you are just looking, so if they want you they will need to offer you more than what you are already getting. They know this as employers. Your skills, no matter what they may be, are needed at some other company at this very minute. All you have to do is go find that company. Treat this like a game of hide-and-seek. You're not looking for a new job because you're angry or because you hate your boss. Tell them the truth. You are looking to make more money to get out of debt. Tell them that you love your job and your boss (I'm guessing that this is true), but the bottom line is that you have set a budget and a goal to get out of debt. So you need to look around to see if you can earn more money with another employer while giving them a hard-working employee. This honesty and go-getting attitude will set most employers back because the average interviewee has no plan or goal. The employer will see someone who can be determined, self-starting, and have a strong reason to work hard to prove themselves. In short, they will love it!

In my current job, I meet and talk with many managers who have employees working under them. They tell me they have a hard time just getting the employees to show up on time, and when they do show up, they work like they don't care. Most employees don't have a goal for their life. You do. You want to get out of debt and start living on 80 percent of what you make. You want to invest for the future. To do this, you are willing to work hard and tackle tough challenges. You have committed to do things that most people find uncomfortable, like looking for a job. Resumes are nice, and they will open doors for you, but you will knock them down when you interview with them. All the things we have talked about so far, if put into practice, will place you far in front of the rest of the applicants.

What Do You Have To Lose? (Part 2)

Once you have completed an application, ask for an interview. Once you have an interview, ask when you might expect to hear from them. If they do not call back when they said they will (this is normal), call them and say, "I was just wanting to stay in touch to see if you have reached any decisions yet. I really like your company and would love to be a part of the team." Pause and let them answer. They will probably put you off for a day or two (this is also normal). Ask them if it would be all right if you called them back later to follow up. Set a time with them before hanging up. This should impress them. At the appointed time, make sure you call, right on time, not a minute late. At this point the employer should be really impressed and should have a better thought as to where they might be able to fit you in. If not, then set another appointment to call back. Do this until they tell you no or they hire you. You have nothing to lose.

Don't put all you eggs in one basket. Keep looking and calling back. Again, I look at it this way: the worst thing that can happen to you at this point is that there would be two companies that would want to hire you, and your current company would want a chance to match the offers. Oh gosh, what a shame. Darn, that has just got to be a terrible problem to have.

See, once you have a positive outlook on this whole possibility, it can be real fun. Think of the interviews and the questions. "What don't you like about your last job?" You could say something like, "Nothing, I like my job." "So why are you here?" and so on. You will just catch them off guard at every corner. They will not have met anyone like you in a long time. Positive, outgoing, self-starting, motivated, goal focused, and ready to go. Holy cow, I'll hire you (kidding). But really, who would not want to have that type of employee working for them? You may not have thought of yourself in these terms before, but take a good look. These are the things you are becoming.

Now get your resume, put on your best clothes, and go get a better job!

8

Part-Time Jobs

Chapter 8:
Part-Time Jobs

I felt a huge responsibility for the debt we had, and I was highly motivated to get rid of it fast. A part-time job was offered to me, working about fifteen hours each week. I took the job and did not mind the work. Each paycheck I held until the bill came from the credit card we were paying off. I cashed the checks, paid my tithe and myself, and the rest went right to the bill, in addition to our regular monthly payment that we would have made anyway. Needless to say, this worked great, and the fourth card was paid off in about six months. That part-time job also ended after six months, but hey, I got a credit card paid off.

Over the course of getting out of debt and staying out of debt. I have held many part-time jobs. Some were project work like waxing floors, cleaning, yard work, teaching guitar lessons, and the like. Some have been regular, traditional part-time jobs. Either way, the paychecks were saved and placed on the next card we were paying off that month.

This seems to be a real simple solution to a hard reality of life, too much debt, but I am stunned at how many people I meet who would rather complain about not being able to pay their bills than go get a part-time job and do something about them.

Sometimes the simplest solutions to problems are the ones right in front of us.

There are always places looking for part-time workers. It does not matter what time you have available; you can find someone looking for part-time help. Late night? Look into Wal-Mart or your local grocery store to be a stock person. Day-time hours? Clean houses. Early morning? Deliver papers. No matter what the time schedule, there is a job out there for you if you look.

Are these jobs going to be fun? Probably not. Are they going to be jobs that you will want to spend forty hours a week doing? Probably not. They are just part-time temporary jobs to help you pay off your debt. You will not be spending the next five years doing this part-time job. If you are married and you do not want to spend time away from your family, remember that it is temporary. My wife and I both had a problem with this, but it was not a permanent job, so we got over it by thinking of the extra time and money we would have very soon. Don't focus on the negative of having a second job. Stay focused on your why and goals. Think about how an extra $100 a month to $100 a week can help you reach your goals.

What you will want to consider:

- How much time will you commit to a part-time job?
- What type of work are you willing to do?
- How much are you willing to make?
- Where should you start looking?

The average person works about eight hours a day. That same average person should get eight hours of sleep a night. With each day having twenty-four hours, that leaves eight hours each weekday and sixteen hours on the weekend to have a part-time job. That is a total of seventy-six hours in your week into which you have to fit a temporary part-time job. You can work a little bit each day or work some longer shifts and get part-time work done in one day like a Saturday.

The message here is that you do have time if you are willing to give it up. Many have told me that they just don't have the time. Well that simply is not true. You have the time; you just don't want too. It would make life hard. You would feel uncomfortable. Your life would have to change. *Yes* to all of that! But so what? *It is just for a short time.* Or do you enjoy living in debt? Are you willing to take twelve years to pay off all your credit cards at minimum payments?

What type of work are you willing to do?

It sure would be nice to have a part-time job doing something we like to do, but don't hold your breath for it. My question to you is this: Does it really matter what you do as a part-time job? The answer here should be no because the job is temporary. Your goal is to get out of debt. This part-time job is just a vehicle to help you get there. Once there, the odds are you will not have this job, so why get hung up on what you will be doing? Focus instead on how much they will pay you to do it.

So much of life is an attitude. Our attitude will either help us or hurt us. Don't look at a job as being below you or not cool for you to do. Instead, look at the much bigger picture. Remember that you are doing this for a big why, your ultimate reason for all this. Don't lose sight of that, and don't think there is a job you don't want to do. There may be jobs that you physically can't do, but don't refuse a job because you don't want to. That would be counterproductive.

How much are you willing to make?

The older I get, the more I realize that my time is valuable. Life is short, and my time is limited. So, for a part-time job, I did not care what I did as long as the money was worthwhile. A six-dollar-an-hour job is not hard to find. Just look at almost any fast-food place. Working about fifteen hours at this each week would bring you ninety dollars. That is about $360 a month for your bills. Now, what about finding a job that pays more? Just like with trading your job up, you should start with something because six dollars an hour beats the zero dollars you'll earn doing nothing. But keep looking and asking around. You just might be surprised what you run into.

Keep your eye open for unexpected offers. I have been asked several times to perform some handyman work around houses. People have asked me what I would charge. Don't be afraid to ask for what you are worth. If they want you bad enough, they will pay what you ask. There is a need around where I live that you might be able to take advantage of. The housing market in my town is very active. Many people everyday are listing their homes with Realtors, but the curb appeal of their house is lacking. In other words, when standing on the road, the house looks bad. Realtors will agree that if the house looks good from the road, the owner will receive more money for the house. There seems to be a job here for someone who would specialize in curb appeal. This could be a part-time job you can demand high dollars for. The current owners will be happy to pay, knowing that they will be able to get more money for their house. After a reputation with Realtors has been built, even more money can be demanded.

Is there a skill you have that you might be able to make into a part-time job? I used my knowledge of the guitar and became a guitar teacher. My friend knows how to clean carpet, so he cleans carpets for others on the weekends. What you do is up to you. Just keep your whys and goals in mind, and many jobs will become fun.

Where should you start looking?

For my wife, the answer to this question was easy. Her employer. The company she worked for was allowing overtime for project work. This was special work that could not, or never was, done during regular hours. She worked early, worked through lunch, and stayed late on three or more nights a week. This was a huge benefit toward our goal. Not only did she work extra hours, but they paid her overtime pay! That, I can tell you, is very nice.

For myself, overtime was not an option. I was paid salary, so there was no extra pay. But there was a traditional part-time job.

If you need some creative help in where to look, here are some suggestions. Start in your own field of work, or try something new. It does not matter. Use the

Internet, help-wanted ads, a staffing agency, signs in store windows, and ask your friends. You never know where the right part-time job might be found. Just get out there and start looking!

No one is going to want to have a second job. They eat into our time and cause all kinds of schedule problems. Having a part-time job means you have two bosses in your life. There are many reasons not to have a part-time job. But, if your why is big enough, there is no problem you will not put up with and work through.

9

Compounding Your Payments

Chapter 9:
Compounding Your Payments

Being a person who lives in Florida, I don't know a whole lot about snow, but I hear snowball fights are a blast—packing the snow to make balls and then sharing that ball of love with a friend or family member, preferably right in the face. Smack! I also hear that to make a snowman you first start with a snowball and then roll it around in the snow. The little ball will gather more snow and become a huge ball. Three of these bigger balls of snow stacked on top of each other makes a snowman.

Now this chapter is not about snow or snowmen, but it is about paying your bills off by using the technique of compounding your payments. Each payment is like a little snowball. We take these payments and throw them at our bills. They have a minor effect on them. But have you ever really thought, "What if I were strong enough to throw that snowman-size snowball? That would have a huge effect on what I am aiming at?" The same theory works with paying your bills. As one bill gets paid off, roll that same payment into another bill's payment. Then, when that bill is paid off, do the same thing by rolling the combined payments into the next credit card bill. By the end, the payment you are making becomes a huge snowman-size snowball. This is what we want to be working toward.

If your budget says you are paying fifty dollars to each of your six credit cards, then when you pay off your first card, take that money and combine it with the next credit card payment to make a new payment of $100. All the other cards would still be paying fifty dollars. If you did this, by the time you got to paying off your last card, you would be mailing in payments of $300 a month. How many months would it take you to pay off your last card at that rate?

Sometimes the answers to our problems come in many different ways. What if you were able to cut the cost of cable out of your budget, saving about forty dollars a month? Then what if you help out a friend with his or her business and make another fifty dollars a month? What if you look at getting a new job and find an offer making fifty cents an hour more, but your current boss matched that and you stayed where you are? Now what would you have at the end of the month to put toward your debt? You saved $40 and earned $50, totaling $90. Earning fifty cents an hour working forty hours a week would be twenty dollars. That would be eighty dollars for the whole month. So the grand total would be $170 to be added to your budgeted monthly payment to pay off your debt.

If you have two car payments, make the higher-interest loan the focus for pay-off. After you have paid that car loan off, combine your two car payments into one, and the second car loan will be paid off very soon.

Many people make the budget mistake of paying off a debt and then spending the money somewhere else. Or they will cut going out to dinner once a month and spend the money on something else, instead. In short, people in general are good at saving money but poor at saving their savings. My older brother stopped smoking and saved the money for a family vacation. He also used to be a bad alcoholic. When he stopped drinking, he saved money. Actually he saved a lot of money due to how much he would drink each week. But he never saved what he saved. He never put the money he was saving away into a real savings account or used it to pay off a debt. So, if you are going to go through all the effort to save some money, be sure to save it!

The difficulty of each debt-escaping technique varies, but this one was the easiest for us to do. It just made sense to us to keep paying out the same level of money each month and compound our payments when one bill was paid off. Our goal was to get out of debt. Our desire was to do this quickly. Because neither one of us liked the tight budget we were on, this budget made life tough.

But we knew that the tighter the budget, the quicker we would be done with our debt.

We also could see that we were used to paying out *X* dollars each month in bills, and if one bill became paid off, why take that money out of our bill paying? We kept the money there and added it to another bill we were paying on. This would certainly help us get out of debt a lot faster, and we were all for that.

There is another way this idea can work for you. At the time of our marriage, my wife and I only had one car. The payment for that car was about $300 each month. When that car was paid off, the other credit card debt was gone, so we decided to keep paying this bill. However, instead of paying this to a car company, we paid ourselves. Each month, we placed into a savings account the sum of $300. We knew that one day we would be in the market for a car, and we should keep the payment going and save for the next car. This did help out when it came time for another car.

10

Kill the Monster Daily

Chapter 10:
Kill the Monster Daily

The lessons and ideas you have read in this book are not revolutionary. There is no magic potion for instant debt-free living to be found here. I have known this for a long time now. So I ask myself why more people don't do this instead of drowning more and more in debt every day, to the point where they can no longer function as a family because every conversation turns to an argument about money. Many reports list money troubles as the leading cause of divorce in America today.

So if the solution is so easy, why is it so hard to do? The monster. The monster is the thing within you that stops you from achieving your greatest potential. For some, the monster is fear—fear of success, fear of change, fear of being responsible, or fear of failure. Fear is a strong monster. What other types of monsters could there be? How about complacency, laziness, busyness, procrastination, lack of desire or urgency, and poor self-esteem, just to name a few? The good news for you is that you are reading this book, so there is some desire to do something about your situation. Now if you can determine your particular monster, then you are almost home.

Take some time and try to figure out what your monster might be. What stops you from greater success? What seems to bog you down when it comes to getting ahead? If you can't identify your monster yourself, I would suggest finding a close and good friend, someone who can tell you the truth no matter what it might be. Ask your friend to help you identify the part of you (which is in all of us) that wants to hold you back. Once you have identified your particular monster, I have but three words of advice for you. This piece of advice could one day be worth a million dollars to you, so be ready, because here it comes. When it comes to your monster,

KILL IT, DAILY!

Here is a plan to help you out:

1. Print a WANTED: DEAD OR ALIVE poster.

2. Organize a posse.

3. Hang the monster.

Print a WANTED: DEAD OR ALIVE poster. What I mean by this is for you to place on paper what it is you are going after: procrastination, fear of change, or whatever is holding you back. Maybe you have many monsters. I would recommend that you place one at a time on the poster. The poster is to be a visual reminder of what you are to *be on the lookout for.* Keep this poster up until you have conquered the monster and then move on to the next target on the most-wanted list. (Sorry for the Western theme, but the kids are having a Western weekend at my house, so it just fit.)

Organize a posse. Once you have a WANTED poster identifying your villain, organize your posse. This would be your friends, family, coworkers, and any others you can recruit to help you spot the villain. If your monster is procrastination, have your friends BOTLO (be on the lookout) for this villain. When they see it, have them point and say something crazy, like "Halt or I'll shoot." Or, if you are in a public place, like a movie line, they could be more discreet and simply point and scream in horror. Your choice. After a few times of some public embarrassment, I bet your thought patterns will begin to change, and you will not have that monster in your life for long.

Hang the monster. Once the monster or villain has been captured in the moment, hang 'em. Don't wait for a trial. Just string up a rope on the nearest tree and let the monster swing in the breeze. Then move on. If necessary, have your friends help you string him up.

Don't let a single day go by without taking a stab at your monster. This is best achieved by action. If it is fear of doing something wrong, replace it with fear of not doing anything at all. If it is complacency, move and take a step every day to make change in your life happen. If it is laziness, get up and get busy. Don't procrastinate. Take action steps each and every day toward your goal. I have a few basic mottos in life that I live by, and here is one:

It is important to know your strengths, but it is more important to know where you are weak.

This is a true statement for everyone in life. If you don't know where you are weak, you can't get better. If you don't know where you are weak, you can't get help in those areas. Learn your weakness so you can become stronger by either getting better in that area or by finding someone who is good at it and having them help you.

Back in the time of Henry Ford, a reporter called him stupid in a newspaper. Mr. Ford took great offense to this and sued the man in court. The defendant's attorney called Mr. Ford to the stand and asked him many questions. The answers he did not know, and he said so. The questions kept coming, but the answer never changed. He simply did not know any of the answers. The attorney said to the courtroom that clearly all could see that Mr. Ford was stupid because he did not know the answers any educated man would know. The judge asked Mr. Ford for his response, and it went something like this: "It is true that I do not know personally any of the answers to the questions I was asked. However, on the desk over there I have a row of switches. Each switch corresponds to a colored light out in the hallway, where I have as many people waiting. If you were to ask me the questions again and I turned on the switch that corresponded with the topic, in would come an expert in the field who would give me the answer to that and many other questions in that topic. If you changed subjects, I would simply change switches, for I do not have time or desire to clutter my mind with wasted trivial knowledge like this. I am an inventor and am focused on that." Needless to say, Ford won the case, and the reporter was made to write an apology in the newspaper.

Sometimes the monster can be a task. This might be something you just hate to do. For me it would be cleaning my desk area. I just hate to go through old papers that have piled up. However, I know that some of them are important, so I can't just blindly throw them all away. The task of going through them one by one is just the hardest thing for me to do. I feel like my time can be better spent doing so many other different things. So this task keeps getting put off and put off again. Then one day I wake up and see a huge pile of paper surrounding my desk. That is the day I know I have to do something about it. So the first thing I do is organize the area. I know this is my monster, and the only way I am going to get it done is to go right at it and do nothing else until I am done. Normally, this takes me all day. But then the monster is dead (at least until the next month, when I have to do it all over again).

Sometimes the monster can be a friend (NOTE: Do not kill your friend! This is for those of you who are literalists.) If your friends are the cause of your distraction, you will need to control your time spent with them. Some friends over my life time have been very destructive for me. These types of friends I recommend losing contact with as soon as possible. They are not helping you, and they surely were not helping me.

Monsters can come in many different shapes and forms. They can be internal or external or both. Each person is different in what and how their monster affects them, but the solution is all the same. Kill the monster. And if necessary, kill it daily.

Yes, this book can and will help you get out of debt and organize your finances. This organization will bring financial freedom and financial firmness to your life and the life of your family. However, whatever your monster is, it will try to delay you, undermine you, and otherwise convince you that you can't do it. Don't let this happen. You can do it. I did it. And others will be doing it too.

11

*A Positive Attitude Is
Not Normal*

Chapter 11:
A Positive Attitude Is Not Normal

For those who have never heard this analogy before, here it goes.

Pour four ounces of water into an eight-ounce glass and then place the glass in front of you. Is the glass now half full or half empty?

In my very early twenties, I read a book called *Think and Grow Rich* by Napoleon Hill. This book had a huge effect on my life at the time. Not because I became rich in my early twenties, because I actually became very poor during that time, spending all the money I made. But this book affected my life by helping me have a positive outlook on life and everything that happens around me. As I was reading the book, I took one suggestion and started putting it into action in my life. Everybody has the standard greeting when you meet them: "Hey, how are you?" "Fine, how about yourself?" "Okay." That's it. Most greetings follow that same simple pattern every day, no matter what is going on in your life. So I started to change my words and found that this was like throwing a wrench into a machine cog. People were caught off guard and surprised. They wondered what happened to me. They wondered if I had won the lotto or something so outrageous that had changed my response in greeting them.

What brought about this type of reaction from my friends? In response to "How are you?" I simply said "Wonderful." That was it. They stopped, looked at me, and wondered why. After about a week of this, I decided to have a little more fun. I expanded my vocabulary to include such words as incredible, super, happy, outstanding, fabulous, and simply marvelous. Needless to say, I received even more stares and weird looks. My friends thought I had lost it. They were half right. I had lost it—not my sanity, however, but my pessimistically numbing outlook on life. Gone were thoughts of the glass as half empty, and I started to see that the glass really was half full, and not just that it was half full, but that I am truly thankful for the half that I have. Many may not even have that much.

With this change of attitude came another change in my life. Daily problems became easier to handle because with every problem came an opportunity to solve it. I found myself enjoying the challenge of solving the problem of the day or week, thinking of how I could solve the problem instead of looking at why it couldn't be done. I never made a million dollars or even half that in my twenties, but that one idea has certainly changed my life. The whole getting-out-of-debt-when-others-say-we-are-stuck idea came from this attitude. I started looking for a way to solve the problem instead of accepting the problem. Currently my problems in life are not over. I face new ones every day, but long gone are the days when the problems would defeat me and run me over. Now I defeat them and enjoy doing it.

Here are two little experiments for you. First fold a single sheet of paper up so that it will fit in your pocket or purse. Carry this with you all day for the next several days. On one side of the paper, write the heading POSITIVE PEOPLE, and on the other side write NEGATIVE PEOPLE. Each time you finish a conversation with someone, take a moment and ask yourself if they had a positive or a negative attitude when they were talking to you. After you have determined which one, place a mark on the corresponding side of the paper you are carrying. Do this for everyone you talk to for several days. After you have spent a few days doing this, you will notice a trend develop. There are more (much more) marks on the negative side than on the positive side.

The second experiment would be for you to fold that paper again so there are two new sides without marks. On one side, mark SUCCESSFUL, and on the other side, mark UNSUCCESSFUL. The next time you find yourself talking with a positive person, ask them if they would describe themselves as generally successful. Guess where the trend goes on this one.

Extra credit: If you choose, and if you are thinking that anyone would rate themselves as generally successful, try this out. Take a full sheet of paper and divide it in half. On the top place the heading POSITIVE, and on the bottom place the heading NEGATIVE. Across the sides on both the top and bottom half, write GENERALLY SUCCESSFUL, MOSTLY SUCCESSFUL, VERY SUCCESSFUL, and EXTRAORDINARILY SUCCESSFUL. When you first talk to someone, determine if they have a positive or negative attitude about themselves. Once you have made your observation, ask them how they see themselves in the following descriptions. Make a mark in the category they fall in, on either the top or the bottom of the page. You will find that positive people will rate themselves as more successful than the negative people. Why do you think this is?

Okay, so you get the point without doing the experiment. What do you do now? Start by changing your attitude. Maybe your monster is that you think negatively. Change your way of thinking. Instead of complaining about a situation, find something positive to say about it. If there is a true problem, there must be a solution just waiting to be found. If this is at your work, your boss will like having someone on the team who is helping to solve the problem instead of complaining about it.

You can change the way you greet someone if you want, but don't lose sight of the bigger picture. The greeting was just the tip of an iceberg, the symptom of a bigger change that was happening within myself. The glass truly was half full, no doubt in my mind. No half-empty thoughts. Just positive, possible, and what-could-be thoughts. That book gave me the million-dollar attitude that has benefited me in everything I have done in my life since that day.

If you had a choice of doing business with someone who is easygoing and positive or with someone who is short answered and overall negative about their life, who would you choose? No one enjoys doing business with a negative person. No one enjoys spending time in a negative environment. Why then would anyone who is successful spend time with someone who is negative and unsuccessful? However, this same person would be more than willing to spend time with someone who is not yet successful but positive. The old saying goes,

"Birds of a Feather Flock Together"

In short, negative attracts negative, and positive attracts positive when it comes to personal relations. If you find yourself around others who are negative, my suggestion is to move them from your close friendship circle and fill the spot with positive friends. Life is too short to spend with friends who drag you down. Your whys are too important to let them keep you from them.

12

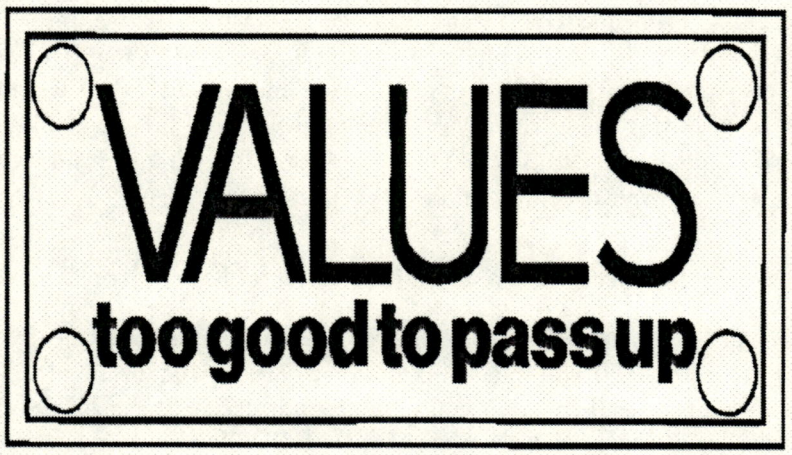

Procrastinate when It Comes to
Spending Money
(Except when It Comes to a Sale!)

Chapter 12:
Procrastinate when It Comes to Spending Money (Except when It Comes to a Sale!)

Most people spend money too easily. If you have the money, you will spend it. How many times have we run out of money before the next payday? Sometimes this is because we have too many bills, and sometimes it is because we can't control our spending. Sometimes it is both. The pace of life is becoming faster by the day. Likewise our spending is striving to keep pace. However, most people run out of money and start using credit and building debt to keep up.

Why is it that we have to keep up with the pace of life by spending more money? Can we keep up without overspending our budgets? Why do we feel we must spend more? Who has been telling us this and why? The questions can be answered partly by turning on the television for just a few minutes. No, TV is not the Antichrist, but it is a vehicle that many companies use to change or modify our thought patterns, telling us that *now* is important, that we deserve better and newer, that bigger is better and faster is greater. Think of all the car commercials that are around. Newspapers, radio, TV, billboards, and flyers are just a few places you will find ads for cars. Why is it that you see so many cars in the used-car lots? Are they broken? Are they no good anymore? Are they unsafe to drive? No, people just wanted to trade in their car for a *new* car with the bigger and better stuff they want to have because they saw it in an ad.

My wife and I have two different thoughts about new cars and how long to keep them. I believe you keep a car until it is unsafe, too expensive to fix, or dead. Then it would be time for a new car. My wife, on the other hand, believes you should get a new car every three years. I asked her why, and in short the answer boils down to *because*. Now my wife is not alone in this thought, because I see thousands of cars in the used-car lots all around town. Obviously many others think just like her.

My thought on buying cars is this: They are a bad investment. You lose value from the moment you sign the papers. It does not matter if you buy new or used. You will always lose money. To trade them when there is still life and safety left in the car is losing even more money. Oh, the car people tell you they will pay off your old vehicle and put you in a new car, but you still owe that money, and the balance transfers to the new car. Just ask a former car salesman. After three years with the same car, is it a little battered? Is it a little stained and dirty? Is it not as nice as the new car at the light next to you? Yes, that is right. It is not. It is three years old, and it is not going to look new anymore. But does that mean they are not any good? No, they are still good and will be good for many more years with a little care. In today's society, we have to have cars to get around, but don't fall into the trap of having to have new all the time. My mother would say this is called being satisfied with what you have. Advertisements create desire, and desire creates dissatisfaction. Learn to be happy with the things you have and put off buying the things you think you want.

Procrastination

Procrastination is a terrible word to me. I can't stand to put things off. Very soon after I have an idea, I start taking action toward that thought. I find myself becoming very impatient with those who procrastinate in life. When it comes to money, procrastination is a wonderful thing. However, I had a huge problem with this when I first tried to procrastinate with money. My problem was that this went against my nature. It was almost impossible for me to not make a purchase I thought was important.

So, remembering my motto,

It is good to know your strengths, but better to know your weaknesses.

I took action toward my problem and developed a holding list for things to buy. This list was for my wife or me to write down things we wanted to buy that were not included in our budget. No purchase was made on any item on this list for fourteen days. This gave me the procrastination time I needed. The list worked out to be a great idea and a huge help. I found out that, on average, one out of three items were things we could live without or could change to something else. We also found that when we place items on a list, we are on the lookout for the place that will offer the best deal. Some items stayed on this list for many weeks until we finally made the purchase.

The new procrastination list was not a hard, fast rule. I remember that one night my wife called me when she was at a department store. They were having a sale on bras. They were two for one, and the regular price was even reduced. This was obviously a great sale, even to me who knows little about bras. I told her to go ahead and purchase as many as she needed. Later that night when we were talking, she told me I had surprised her with that comment. I asked why. She said I had never done that before, and I said yes to spending money on something that was not even on the list yet. I reminded her that we had talked about buying some new bras for her, but they had not yet made the list. I also asked her about how good the deal was. She informed me again that she had only rarely seen this make of bras that low, so I told her we really did need them and that the expense would have been coming. The sale was great, and to wait would be to spend more money in just a couple of weeks. That did not make sense. It's not like she did not need them and noticed a great sale. In that case, I would have said no. But she did need them, and they were having a great sale, so why wait?

Just yesterday as I was writing this book, I discovered I needed jumper cables around my house. I knew that one day soon I would go buy them, but I didn't know where I should buy them, so I procrastinated. Long ago I would not have been able to go to sleep that first night if I had not gone out and solved the problem. Now the waiting is paying off. Today I went to pick up a used truck I purchased from a friend who was moving out of state. As I was driving home, I glanced behind the passenger seat, and there was a set of jumper cables. No need now to go buy them. Procrastination, when it comes to spending money, pays off!

So how can you apply this to your life? Step one: make a money procrastination list. Write that at the top of the page and make lots of blank lines for you to write down the things you think you need. Step two: place this list in a spot that is good for you to look at once in a while but not every day. I put mine with my bills. Step three: when you think of something you need, write it down on the list. Put a date before the item of when you placed it on the list. This will help you keep track of how long it has been on the list. Step four: while you are procrastinating about spending money, go and look for the best place to purchase the item. Who will have the best deal on what you are looking for? As money becomes available in your budget, go to your list and start at the top. If the first line is still very important to you and you have the money, go and make that purchase. If not, go ahead to the next item. If you pass over an item twice for something else down the list, scratch it off the list. Obviously this item is no longer of importance to you at this time.

It sounds funny to say that not spending money saves you money, and it saves your budget. At the end of one year, just look at your list and realize the number of items on the list that are no longer important to you. In the old days, you would have run out and made the purchase, and now you don't even need the item anymore. This impulsive, got-to-have-it-now society that we live in feeds this desire within us. Don't let that feeling win and ruin your budget.

Reality check, please. I am assuming that if a great sale, never to be repeated again, comes along and you don't have the money, then you need to not make a purchase. If you place an item on your procrastination list and wait fourteen days but still don't have the money, don't go buy the item just because you waited. Purchase the item when you have the money and you have found the best deal. Don't look for loopholes or try to find ways around this whole budget thing. Neither I, nor anyone else, is making you do this budget. You have to decide to do it for yourself. And remember this:

The tighter the budget,
the quicker you get out of debt.
The tighter the budget,
the more you are motivated to get out of debt.

13

Wants, Needs, and Desires

Chapter 13:
Wants, Needs, and Desires

In this chapter, I will spend a moment and define three little words that will help you successfully live within your budget and your procrastinating shopping list. The words to remember are

WANTS, NEEDS, AND DESIRES

These three words are the basic categories for everything in life that we buy. Food is definitely a need. Ice cream, although in the food category, would have to fall under the want category (unless you are dealing with a pregnant wife; then it is *a must*). Let's look a little more closely at what I mean.

WANTS: Wants are things we would *like to have* now, but we have no strong passion for this item. The key words here are *like to have*, not things we have to have for work, or gas for our cars, but more like gum at the checkout line or a five-dollar car wash after a fill-up. These are just things we will from time to time *want*. But do we really *need* them? Are they a necessity? Can we live without them until we save up for them? My point is that wants are not necessary, and we can live without them. When the money and budget say you can splurge a little for being good, have at it. Go buy a super-sized dessert at your favorite restaurant. But on the day-to-day and week-to-week bases, don't buy your wants!

NEEDS: Needs are the things you have to have to make it through. This category is easy to understand and hard to not cheat in. For example, food is a need, but McDonald's—though to some people is a special food group—is not a need. Cigarettes—are you addicted to them? If yes, then get help. If you're not addicted to them and you say, "Oh, I could quit anytime," then quit, and this is not a need. (Same with beer.) How about dog food? Yes, if you have a dog. However, canned dog food? No, dry dog food will be fine. Don't let your pet keep you in the poorhouse. Shoes are definitely a need. However, if the ones you are wearing are still good, then wait and put this on your procrastination list and save for them.

DESIRES: Desires are things we would *like to have now*, and there is a strong passion for this item. Not with my kids, but I have noticed the perfect example with someone else's kids. While in a grocery store, a family heads toward the checkout line. The little kid picks up some small piece of candy with her favorite cartoon creature on it. The mom says no, and the kid goes into the tantrum from hell, like you were going to pull her teeth out if she did not get the item right then. Loud would not describe the volume level the kid reaches as she exclaims how much she must have the item. Now that is desire. Need it? Nope. But you have a strong passion for it, now. For me it would be a tool from my favorite tool store. For my wife it would be a cooking gadget for the kitchen. For my daughter, well, she does not get a vote. Anyway, watch out for the desires. Most of the desires that go on my list are not purchased in the end. Many of the wants are, but not many of the desires. Desires I save as a reward for reaching really hard goals.

The procrastination list is great for controlling and filtering the wants, needs, and desires. Learning to identify what category each item you are looking to purchase falls into is not hard. With a little bit of thought, you will soon be able to identify very quickly where each item falls within these categories.

Make a third column on your procrastination list. Title this column W, N, D. This stands for wants, needs, and desires. As you place an item on this list, also make a determination as to what category it falls into. Needs will be items you purchase first. Sometimes you may not be able to wait the two weeks for these purchases. That's okay. Just do your best. Wants and desires must wait the two-week or longer time period. This will allow you to save up or prioritize your spending to fit it into your budget. Also remember that this is the time you want to find the best deal on what you are looking to purchase.

So how does all this mental categorizing help me to stay within my budget? Good question. Many purchases I used to make on a regular basis I thought were all part of my needs for life. But they were not. They were wants and desires. When I focus my financial resources on buying the needs and procrastinate the wants and desires, I not only feel better about my finances, but when I do make a purchase for a want or a desire, I feel great. There is more value found because of the sacrifices made along the way. I pay cash, so I don't have to worry about the long-term debt hanging over my head.

Over the last several weeks, my wife and I have been discussing the purchase of an entertainment center. This would help out the clutter in our living room and add to the overall beauty of the house. We definitely understand that this is not a need. It is definitely something we want, but for us it falls more in the desire category. So, after several days of talking this over, I had a thought. For over a year we have talked about having a garage sale and cleaning out some of our junk. Why not have a garage sale and put the money raised toward the new purchase? So that is what we are doing. Also, I picked up a one-time job of helping a family move into their new house and made a few bucks. This money will also go toward the new piece of furniture. In the end we will gain a desire without affecting our budget. Plus we gain a cleaner garage. Life is great!

The Best Valentine Present Ever

It all started the weekend after Christmas. We were walking through a large department store, looking for the bargains found during the after Christmas sales. Before we started we had looked over our procrastination list and knew we could buy a few items given our current budget. While walking down the closeout aisle, my wife stopped short with a gasp. "What's wrong?" I asked. She pointed and began to tell me how much she had always wanted a Kitchen Aid countertop mixer. "So why the sudden stop?" I asked. Then I got the fifteen-minute story of all the times she had priced them and where. She told me what the best price she had ever found was, and the closeout was twenty dollars under that. She was excited. (NOTE: This is the reaction of a desire.) I told her calmly that this was not on our list or within our budget, so she sighed and we moved on. That night I thought about all she had told me. The next day my friend called me to help him with a quick side job. No problem. I spent most of the day helping him and made fifty dollars in cash. On the way home, I stopped by the store and put the item on lay away. Because it was a closeout from Christmas, they only gave me forty-five days to pick it up. With some calls made over the next couple of days, I found several little jobs I could do making all but forty dollars of the Kitchen Aid. Now I just had to come up with when to give it to my wife. While looking at the calendar, I noticed that Valentine's Day was coming in just a few weeks, so I had the idea of giving it to her on that day. I thought I was running the risk of offending her by this. You know, the most romantic day for a couple, and I give her a kitchen appliance. Something did not sound right to me, but I took the chance. It seemed like she really wanted it with a huge desire.

The big day was here. Over the last couple of paychecks, I had scheduled the money needed to pay it off, but that was it. There was no money for a card, flowers, or even wrapping paper. I brought the gift home and placed it on the dining table. She was going to be home in about fifteen minutes, so I grabbed a blanket to cover the box.

The moment arrived. She was home and looking at the blanket-covered box on the dining room table and at me. I told her I loved her and that here was her present. "Sorry I did not have the money to wrap it, but I hope you will understand in a minute." Not sure what to think, she cautiously lifted the blanket. Once her eyes caught a glimpse of the box, a high-pitched scream flew, and so did the blanket. Next flowed words of great joy about how she had always wanted a Kitchen Aid. That lasted for about fifteen minutes. While this was going on, she dug into the box to revel in every little item that came with the mixer. After the excitement calmed down and she had gone through the entire box, I got a kiss and was told very assuredly that this was by far the best present she had ever received on Valentine's Day.

The point of this story is not to blow your budget on desires. Work extra and save. They will mean more when you have them. It meant more for my wife.

14

Rewards for Your Successes

Chapter 14:
Rewards for Your Successes

Gratification is a huge motivator for all people. Advertisers know this and play on our desires. They tell us to have it our way and to have it now. We deserve it. We've earned it. This is why most food stores place candy bars at the checkout line, to give us that instant gratification and the rush of chocolate. This, however, will kill both our diet and our desire to spend less so we can get out of debt. The majority of the rewarding advertised all around us is only going to benefit the manufacturer and seller of the product, not us. So why do we give in so easily? Because there is a huge lack of education today on what rewards and gratification should be, and the first lesson is that it is not instant!

Instant is good for some things, like coffee and service at the drivers-licensing agency, but instant gratification is not good at all. Where is the pride in that? Where is the feeling you get when you have earned something through hard work and sacrifice? This is an attitude we must break to be successful at living within 80 percent of our income.

I had a rough first year at my first sales job when I was learning how to sell. I finally got it down around the six-month mark on the job. But for the next six months, I could not figure out why I wasn't getting better. Then, while reading a book on success, I learned about setting goals and rewards. For large goals, I learned to set large rewards. For small goals, I learned to set small rewards. I could not figure out my problem. I had a list of large goals. Along with that list was a large list of rewards. These rewards were way out of my affordability, but if I hit my sales goals, I could easily afford them. But there was a problem. I could not hit my goals. Then I remembered something about small goals. I enjoyed this little soft-serve yogurt shop nearby, so I set a goal that I would not have another yogurt until I made one sale. The next day I had a sale and a peanut butter yogurt (a personal favorite.) The next day I had another because I made another sale. This was great. Make a sale and have a yogurt. I loved this. That month, needless to say, I had a bunch of yogurts. I also hit a larger goal on my list.

I stopped swinging for the fence and started with step-by-step goals, and by the end of the month I had hit a home run. I learned that smaller bite-size goals are as important, if not more important, than larger goals. The small goals, when put together, will allow you to get to a larger goal. That was the lesson I learned by the end of my first year in sales. I'm sorry I did not learn that in the beginning.

So we have talked about setting goals, large hard-to-reach goals and smaller goals to help you get there. Now I want you to start thinking about what you can reward yourself or yourselves with when you achieve them. For the small goals, make it also small rewards, a reward you will enjoy and that is not expensive. For me this would have something to do with food. For my brother, his small goal would have something to do with exercise or golf at a special place. My wife would enjoy having her car taken to a car wash. Small, simple rewards for small goals.

Take a sheet of paper and write down at the top a major goal you would like to achieve. This could be paying off a credit card or paying off a personal loan. Think of a huge reward you will place with that event when it happens, like a celebration dinner at a fancy restaurant or whatever. Now take some time and make three smaller goals that will help you achieve the larger goal. What are three steps you will need to take before you get to the last and final step? If your large goal was to pay off a credit card, some smaller goals would be to find ways to do this—another part-time job, trading up jobs, or another idea found here in this book. Then attach a small reward for each one achieved.

Not all goals have to cost money. Someone once challenged me to plan and hold an event for twenty-five people and only spend one dollar. I took the challenge and found that this can be done. It just takes more thinking on how to get it done. So not all goals, large or small, need to cost money. One thing my family likes to do is go to Downtown Disney. This day trip costs gas and lunch. That's it. There are many things you can do that would cost very little. I suggest you focus on some of these "no-money" events at first while you are looking to get totally out of debt.

Here are some events or rewards that you can do for less than ten dollars:

- Invite your friends to your house for a party and have them bring food and drinks.
- Invite a couple of friends over for cards.
- Go to the dollar movie theater.
- Go spend a day at a state park.
- Go to the beach.

Now for the larger rewards for meeting the larger goals. A former boss several years ago gave me some advice on this. To my surprise, he was right. I had just won a contest prize that was a gift card at a local electronics store. My wife and I were just coming out of debt, and we were thinking we could use this gift card to get some of the needed items on our procrastination list. My boss said I should use the money on things I would never take my own money and buy. He told me to seek out items in the store I didn't need but would definitely like, things I didn't even have a desire for because they were too out of my range of reality. So I talked it over with my wife, and we thought this made sense. We went shopping and got some great stuff. Just a few months later, I won another sales contest. The prize was another gift card to the same electronics store. We went shopping again, this time without any prompting from my boss. This happened two more times that same year. Today my wife and I sit in our living room and point to almost everything and say, "Won that." The items included a TV, a VCR, ceiling fans, a washer, a deep freezer (okay, this item is not in the living room), camping gear, boom boxes, and a BBQ grill, just to name a few.

Now this was possible because my bosses created the contests with the prizes. But the principle will work for the larger goals in your life. As a matter of fact, they have for me. Many of the larger desires that my wife and I both want become attached to a large goal. This keeps us both focused and supportive of each other.

Here are some events or items that we have used as larger rewards:

- Purchased tickets to Walt Disney World
- Purchased a new car
- Ate dinner at a very fancy restaurant
- Bought a dog
- Added a larger back porch to our home
- Added a screen cage to our back porch
- Purchased yearly family passes to the zoo

We had this idea to increase the size of our back porch and have the new, larger porch screened in. This was something that both my wife and I were very excited about doing, so we placed this on our procrastination list and waited. We decided we would set a large goal for this reward. Our goal was to be at a specific place with our finances and debt before we did it. Also, we must have the money for it in the bank. We knew we were not going to save up to do it all in one year, so we decided to make the reward just adding onto the porch first. Time passed and we worked hard at our finances. Later that year we reached our goal and looked to add the porch.

The next year we did the same thing for the screen to be added. This was a wonderful way of doing this. We bit off exactly what we could chew at that time, and we did it. The reward was tangible and not something we would do every day. It also improved the value of our home in the process. In pricing out the screen porch, we found a great deal we could not refuse. In short, we got the screen porch for about half price from the best company in town due to a friend-of-a-friend relationship. Because we were not expecting this after the screening was done, we had money left over, so the family packed up and went shopping for some patio furniture. Now this is the benefit of procrastinating buying and setting goals with rewards.

15

Invest Your Savings

Chapter 15:
Invest Your Savings

Some friends have asked me, "While in debt, should you use the 10 percent set aside for savings to pay down debt?" My answer for this is "No, not at all!" Your savings are for your long-term life. Once you have drawn your financial line in the sand, there is no going back. Your financial outlook on life is changing so that you will live on 80 percent of your income. Once you have started saving 10 percent, don't stop or use that money for anything else.

Here is the one exception to the rule of not using your long-term savings: Buying a home. If you are going to purchase a home and you need money for your down payment, this is a great spot to use your long-term savings. Homes are a great investment. If you have a home and are looking to upgrade to a larger one, this would be a great area to invest your long-term savings.

When is buying a home a bad deal? When you pay too much. How do you know if you got a great deal? Work with a Realtor and do some calculations yourself. Finding a good Realtor is not that hard. Finding a great one takes some time. Spend as much time as it takes for you to find someone you are comfortable with. After you have found a home you are interested in placing an offer on, ask your Realtor to give you a report on comparable properties in the same subdivision that have sold in the last six months. Study this report, comparing dollars paid per square foot, features (updated, pool, two-car garage, etc.), average sell to average list price, and any other factors on the house. This should give you a great idea on what to offer the seller for the house you are interested in.

So why is placing your long-term savings into a house a good investment? One reason is that your money would be hard to access and spend on a want or a desire. Second, houses over the years have proven to be a safe investment. Third, depending on where you purchase, you will make a great return on your investment when you sell. There are many tax benefits to owning your own home, and I advise you to have a good accountant help you take advantage of all that is allowed by law.

Other possible places for your savings:

- Your home
- Mutual funds
- IRA's or any tax-benefiting accounts
- Savings accounts

- Certificate of deposits (CDs)

- Bonds

- Others

It is not so much where you place your money as it is following these three guidelines:

1. **Place your money.** Don't let it sit without earning interest somewhere.

2. **Review each possible place for security**. This is your savings, and you don't want to lose it to someone who is committing fraud. Check out each possibility many different ways. If it sounds too good, run!

3. **Be consistent.** Add to your investment each payday. Take your 10 percent by writing a check to get the money out of your checking account. Do this each time you get paid, and watch the money pile up over time. The longer it earns interest, the more you will have.

Many years ago when we started to turn our finances around, we placed our 10 percent into a savings account. By the end of the first year, I was a little nervous because there started to be a nice amount of money sitting within a short distance of my reach at my local bank. So at the beginning of the new year, I pulled the money out and sent it to our choice for an investment company. This was the same company that my father-in-law has used for many years and has had great returns over those years. So this started us with two areas of savings. Each year, as we look at our savings, we send money from our local account to our investment company for them to place in mutual funds.

I know I have written about this before, but it is definitely worth writing about again. The third way we have our savings is through my wife's employer-matched 401(k) funds. This is a winner in so many ways.

- **Funds go in before taxes.**

- **The employer matches currently up to 6 percent out of 10 percent going in (that's a gain of 60 percent right off the bat).**

- **The fund is compounding earnings every day.**

- **There is never a week that we don't invest because the employer does it for us out of her check.**

If you have the opportunity to do this, I highly recommend it. So now is the time for you to do something. If you currently have your employer taking funds out, make sure it is the maximum you can take out, up to 10 percent of your pay.

IF you do not already have a savings program started, this is the time to start one. I suggest you place your first savings into a savings account. Keep placing it there until you have about two months of living expenses in the account. While this is building up, start looking for the next place you wish to place the money. You might want to consider a mutual fund. Set a goal to reach a certain amount, and send your money there. Once that goal is reached, have another place or fund you would like to invest in.

The goal here is to not have all your eggs in one basket. Don't invest all your long-term savings in one mutual fund or type of savings account. You want to have many different types of accounts. This will help protect you from wild turns in the economy. I am looking to have three types of mutual funds. They are as follows: conservative investments, moderately aggressive investments, and very risky investments. I will not have my money divided equally, but I will have some money in each type of fund. The main goal is to be consistent, regularly placing money into these accounts. That is what will make you financially well off in the years to come.

16

Good Debt Defined

Chapter 16:
Good Debt Defined

Is there any debt that is good? Yes. I will tell you about a few types here. I have already mentioned that a home is a good thing to have, and this would be a good debt. Why? Because the interest is tax deductible! That is awesome! I had no idea how big a difference this would make on my taxes, but after we received our tax refund from that first year as a homeowner, we were able to have fewer taxes taken out of our paychecks. Life is good!

In the beginning of this book, I told you how bad a situation my wife and I started off in. Her credit score was awful. After we were out of debt (or close to the end), we signed up for a credit card in her name. It had only a $200 limit. We went out and made a purchase or two and then hid the card away. We took our time paying this card off (about three or four months). Then we pulled the card back out again and charged some more items that were wants. After that, we spent the next several months paying the card off again. Soon after that, the credit card company raised the limit to about $500 for her card. We took the card and went out and charged a little more (higher than the last two times), and then worked on paying the card off. Well, in short, in about a year and a half that card reached a $1,000 credit limit. Other card offers came in with better interest rates, no fees, and other conveniences, so my wife has another card. We just canceled the first credit card. So why was this good debt? Good question. My wife's credit score was very low. We needed to raise her score so we could buy a house. This first credit company took a chance with her, and we were faithful in our payments. Her score came up. The more they increased her card, the more we stretched our temporary debt and paid it off. This helped her score again. After about three years of marriage, we were out of debt and buying our new home. About a year after that, we purchased our first new car.

Let me talk about this new car and how this is a good debt. Interest rates were going way down, and many car manufacturers were having low offers on interest rates. We bought our first new car at a 3.9 percent interest rate. I thought that was the best thing that could have happened to us, until about one year later when my personal car reached 100,000 miles and we needed a new car. Then the same car manufacturer was offering new cars with a 0.0 percent interest rate for those who qualified. We did, and that's like free money. I call that a good debt. Using someone else's money for five years and paying no interest. SWEET!

These types of deals are rare. Remember to always read the fine print. Look for the hidden charges or the catch. If there are none, then it's going to be a great deal. If there are charges or hidden fees, don't do it. For example, I have always been told that when the interest rates on my home loan drop more then 1.5 percent, I should refinance. They say this would save me huge amounts of money. I did not take my own advice. I refinanced without looking at all sides of the issue. About two years after I had refinanced, the loan balance of my house was the same. After two years, I had not moved below where I was because of all the closing fees. Considering that the average person only lives in a house for about five years, I will never make this up to the point I could have been at without refinancing. Bad debt! So look for the fine print and make the best decision you can.

Do you have any good debt? If so, leave it alone. Focus on the bad debt. I pay nothing extra on any of my car loans. Why? It is almost totally free money. As for my house loan, I make one or two extra payments to principle each year. This amount is equal to a full regular house payment. I stay focused on paying off bad debt and investing my long-term savings.

What about some furniture store offering no interest for three years if you purchase this weekend? I have seen two types of these advertisements. One is a sale, and you get the 0 percent financing. With the other, you just get the 0 percent. I would rather save money on the actual purchase and pay it off soon than pay full price and have 0 percent interest.

I don't recommend going into debt as a rule. Some debt is unavoidable and expected, like car loans and your home loan, but a loan for a couch? I don't know about that. I would personally do it this way. Say my wife and I wanted new bedroom furniture—nice dressers, matching nightstands, side chairs, headboard, and so on. You know, the works. The sale is going on now, and it is with no interest for three years. Because we have worked hard on our budget, we have freed up about $300 each month. We would make the purchase and pay this money each month until it was paid off.

You might wonder, "Why pay it off if it truly is 0 percent interest? Well, my answer would simply be, "Because it is an extra." This purchase is a desire, not a need. Don't tie up your available credit for desires. What if during this time something went wrong with our home and we had to make an expensive repair? You might just need the room in your credit sometime during those three years. Don't tie up your credit on desires. That would be bad.

Another good-and-bad-debt item to consider is with credit cards. Credit card companies are offering not only low rates but also incentives for you to have their card in your wallet. This can be an evil thing or a great thing for you. It all depends on how you handle the card. If you are able to charge items on the card and pay it off at the end of the month and receive the rewards, this is a great deal.

If you are not, then the company has just suckered you, and you're back into debt.

My father-in-law has a card that offers cash off his next new car purchase. This money discount is based on each month's purchases, so he pays for all his regular household expenses with this card instead of paying cash. When the statement comes in, he simply writes one big check and pays it off each month. This has worked out very well for him.

Some companies offer other free items or discounts. I wanted to look into this to find one for our family to benefit from. Each year we take a vacation through a time-share travel club. This club has a membership fee. They offer a credit card that has the benefit of no fee for your membership. I called to find out more information. The news was not good. There were limits on how much I could earn, and if we fell below a certain amount we would be charged for our membership dues. This sounded awful. It seemed like there was no way to win with this card company, so we now have a card that earns us money off the next new car we purchase.

17

Trash
Your
Debt
(Part 2)

Chapter 17:
Trash Your Debt (Part 2)

At this point, you might be having second thoughts. Your head may be swimming with thoughts like, "There are just too many things to do. I can't do it." And so you don't. Fight this thought. Remember, you are not expected to do everything at once. Just take one idea at a time. Set your short-term goal as one per week. If you fail to do one this week, then next week set a goal to get that one goal done. Then move on to the next goal on your list. You did not get into debt overnight, and you surely won't get out of debt overnight either. It takes some time. Short of winning the lottery or someone giving you a check for $50,000 out of the blue, you will not get out of debt overnight. There is no quick fix. You have to work at these principles to be able to climb out and stay out of debt. These principles will not only help you to get out and stay out, but they are laying a foundation you can build on, like starting your own business or building new income avenues in your life, allowing your financial bathtub to overflow like a river. When this happens, your whys will be within reach, and they will become your reality.

Many never reach this point in their lives. It is said that the average person has over $9,000 in consumer debt. That would be $18,000 per couple. The average household savings is about 3 percent of their income. We as a society are running fast toward our retirement age and not saving for it now. There will be a huge surprise for some. For others there will be a huge reward.

So what will you do? Have you started already? Can you relate to my life when I was buried in a mountain of debt? Are you ready to get out? Remember that getting out takes hard work and effort on your part. Remember that it does not happen overnight, but once it does, the momentum will build and build. That momentum will continue to build as long as you keep doing the little things that started your financial recovery. After a year or two past being out of debt, you will look back and wonder how you got to where you are in your finances. Your look will be one of total amazement.

Remember, I said in the beginning that this is not a get-rich-quick book. I also said this is not a get-out-of-debt-in-ten-easy-steps book. This is a book of sound principles, and all that needs to be added is a little work. Some effort will be easy, and some will be most difficult. I thought living without cable TV would be hard. Now I hardly miss it. Many things that need to go away in your life will be just like that. You won't miss them at all. You will begin to focus on why you are doing this and how you will get there. Then you will see that many things in our lives that slow us down and keep us in debt are just things, and things we can live without.

18

Imagine—For the Few Who Are Ready to Get out of Their Jobs and Retire Early.

Chapter 18:
Imagine—For the Few Who Are Ready to Get out of Their Jobs and Retire Early.

Everyday it's the same. Get up, go to work, come home, go to bed, and repeat the next day. This is the life of most. Most of us work for someone else, allowing them to do the things we wish we could be doing while we work for them. Something is wrong with this picture. I want to be the one who receives money while I sleep and vacation in the islands. I want to work at a job I like to do and not worry about the money. I want to see this great country of ours without the limits of a two-week vacation. I am ready for this life. Are you?

Imagine your life and what it would be like if money just showed up every week in your bank account. Imagine that this happens each week with or without you doing anything for it. Imagine that this flow of money never stopped and that it would still be there for your grandchildren and great grandchildren. Wow, now that is something I want in my life. How about you? Really? Are you sure? Are you ready for this? Are you willing to work hard now to get this money flow started? We're not talking about winning the lottery or starting a multilevel marketing (MLM) thing and becoming a huge overnight success. We are talking about developing real cash flows that will overflow your life so much it will flow into the lives of others.

The next book will chronicle the steps I have taken to become financially wealthy. Just like this book, there will be much you will have to do, but the steps will be attainable for you and anyone else who wishes to go this far. However, let me warn you by sharing with you one more of my mottos:

With much freedom comes much responsibility.

Let me explain this if you are unsure how it applies here. As those who are given much (i.e., money), we have a responsibility or trust to see that it is not abused and that it is used for the betterment of others, while enjoying our part of course. But we are not to horde it away and fail to share the blessings given to us with others.

While I'm on this subject, that goes for this book. If you find a financial difference in your life because of this book, then great; share it with a friend. How many of your friends are in the same debt boat as you are or were? Don't hide this information. Tell others. Help save them from the death grip of debt. Share what is given to you in this book and what you enjoy. Many people will be just fine using and applying the lessons of this book in their lives and will not go on to study the next book. That is just fine. Not everyone is ready for great wealth. There is much to consider before undertaking this adventure, like knowing who you are and why you are truly going to this next level. If you are just after money for the sake of having money, I would suggest to you that you will not make it. I also would suggest that you should read someone else's book on how to get there, because my book will not help you at all. But if you are ready, are sure of who you are and why you are doing this, and are willing to share your success with others, then I am ready for you.

For now, work on getting out of debt, living within 80 percent of your income, saving 10 percent, and giving away 10 percent. Take care and God bless!

The Line in the Sand

Finding out where you are financially

Debts	Balance owed	Interest rate	Available credit	
Credit card 1				
Credit card 2				
Credit card 3				
Credit card 4				
Credit card 5				
Car loan 1				
Car loan 2				
Home loan				
Line of credit				
Other				
Fixed monthly bills	Current	Estimate 1	Estimate 2	Estimate 3
Power/electric				
Water/sewer				
Day care				
Cell phone				
Insurance—car				
Tithing/donations				
Insurance—home/renters				

House phone/long distance				
Cable/Internet				
Variable monthly bills				
Food				
Pet care				
Dining out				
Gas				
Assets	Value			
Item 1				
Item 2				
Income				
Job 1				
Job 2				
Other 1				
Other 2				

My Monthly Budget Worksheet

Tithe					
Savings					
Day care					
Mortgage					
Time share					
Car repair/ new car					
Kids' college fund					
House repair					
Insurance					
Phone					
Electric					
Kids' school lunch					
Water bill					
Cell phone					
Charge card 1					
Charge card 2					
Charge card 3					
Charge card 4					
Spouse's card 1					
Spouse's card 2					

Interest Rate Comparison Chart

Credit Cards	Balance Owed	Available Balance	Interest Rate	Minimum Payment Due
Visa 1				
Visa 2				
Visa 3				
Master Card 1				
Master Card 2				
Master Card 3				
American Express				
Other				
Other				

Resources

Web listings that you might find helpful

www.trashyourdebt.com
www.equifax.com
www.uslegalforms.com
www.pueblo.gsa.gov (Look under *money*.)

0-595-33723-6

Printed in the United States
51150LVS00006B/94